ORGAN

THE BEST SONGS EVER

ISBN 0-7935-3544-1

HAL•LEONARD®
CORPORATION

7777 W. BLUEMOUND RD. P.O. BOX 13819 MILWAUKEE, WI 53213

THE BEST SONGS EVER

All I Ask Of You
from THE PHANTOM OF THE OPERA

Electronic Organs

Upper: Flutes (or Tibias) 16', 8', 4'
Lower: Melodia 8', Reed 8'
Pedal: 8'
Vib./Trem.: On, Fast

Drawbar Organs

Upper: 80 4800 00
Lower: (00) 7334 011
Pedal: 15
Vib./Trem.: On, Fast

Music by Andrew Lloyd Webber
Lyrics by Charles Hart
Additional Lyrics by Richard Stilgoe

Slowly, with feeling

RAOUL

No more talk of dark - ness, for let
Let me be your free - dom, let

get these wide - eyed fears; I'm here,
day - light dry your tears;

I'm here, noth - ing can harm you,
here, with you, be - side you, my

CHRISTINE

words will warm and calm you.
guard you and to guide you.

All I ask is eve - ry wak - ing mo - ment,

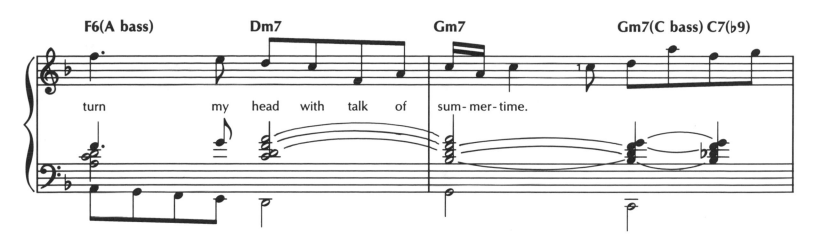

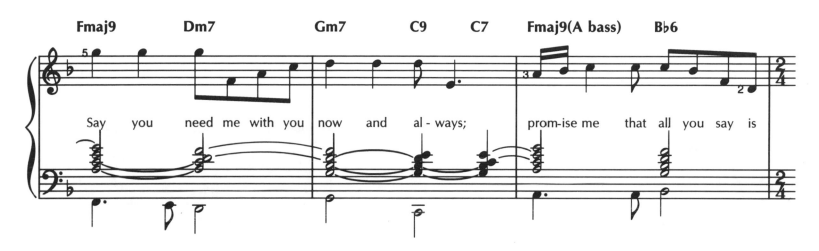

6

CHRISTINE

fears are far be - hind you. All I want is free - dom, a world with no more night; and

you, al - ways be - side me, to hold me and to hide me. Then

RAOUL

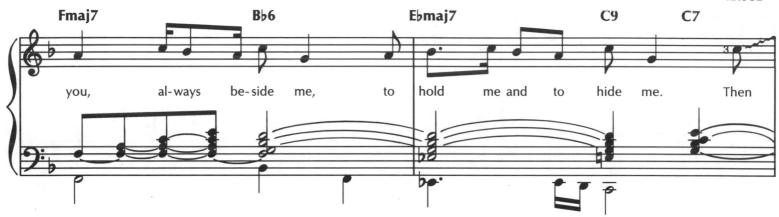

say you'll share with me one love, one life - time; let me lead you from your

sol - i - tude. Say___ you___ need me with you,

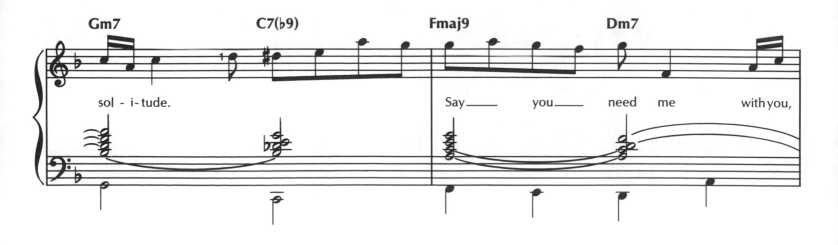

All The Things You Are

from VERY WARM FOR MAY

Electronic Organs
Upper: Oboe 8′
Lower: Flute 8′, Diapason 8′
Pedal: 8′
Vib./Trem.: On, Fast

Tonebar Organs
Upper: 50 7232 000
Lower: (00) 8301 000
Pedal: 25
Vib./Trem.: On, Fast

Lyrics by Oscar Hammerstein II
Music by Jerome Kern

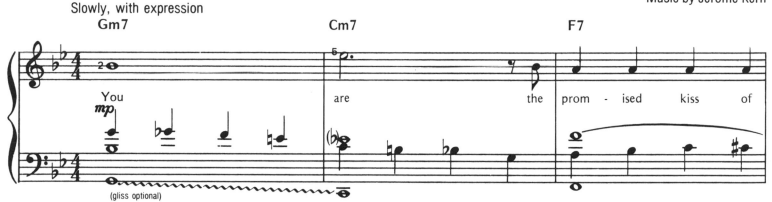

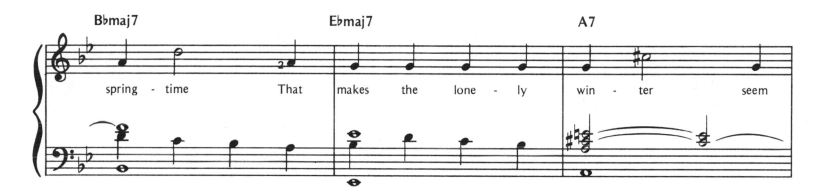

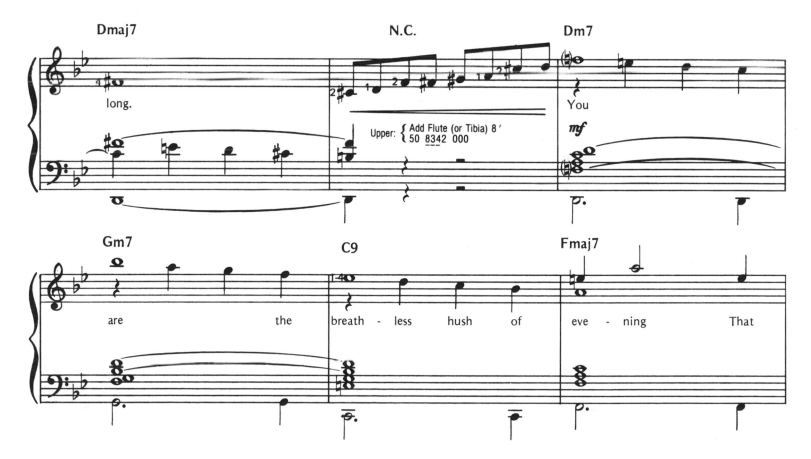

B♭maj7 ... **E7** ... **Amaj7**

trem - bles on the brink of a love - ly song.

N.C. ... Slightly Faster **Bm7**

You __ are __ the __ an - gel glow __

Upper: { Add Clarinet
54 8342 000
cresc.

17

f

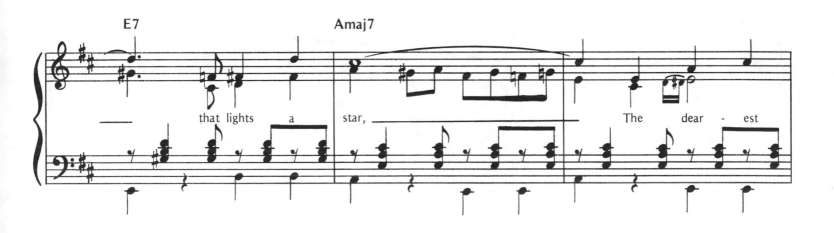

E7 ... **Amaj7**

that lights a star, __ The dear - est

Bm7 ... **Bdim N.C.** ... **G♭**

things I know __ are what you are.

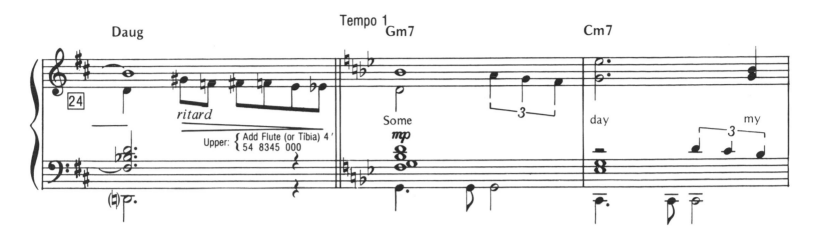

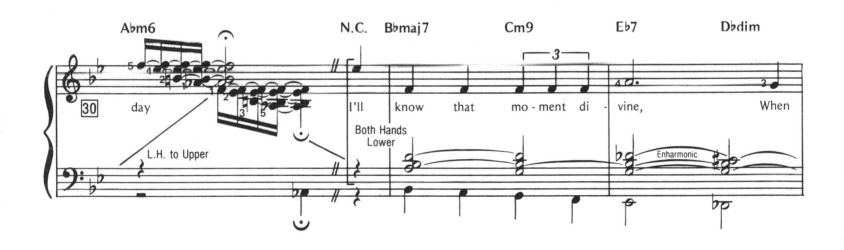

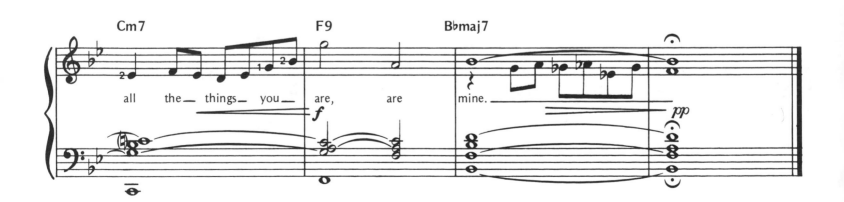

Always

Electronic Organs

Upper: Flutes (or Tibias) 8', 2', String 8'
Lower: String 8', Diapason 8'
Pedal: 16'
Vib./Trem.: On, Fast

Drawbar Organs

Upper: 00 8386 430
Lower: (00) 4464 443
Pedal: 4 2
Vib./Trem.: On, Fast

Words and Music by
Irving Berlin

Ev - 'ry - thing went wrong,
Dreams will all come true,

and the whole day
grow - ing old day with

long
you

I'd
And

feel
time

so
will

blue.
fly.

For the long - est
Car - ing each day

while,
mare,

I'd for - get to
Than the day to be -

smile
fore

Then
Till

Blue Skies

Electronic Organs

Upper: Flutes (or Tibias) 8', 2', Clarinet
Lower: Flute 4', Diapason 8', String 8'
Pedal: String Bass
Vib./Trem.: On, Fast

Drawbar Organs

Upper: 00 8383 833
Lower: (00) 5555 330
Pedal: String Bass
Vib./Trem.: On, Fast

Words and Music by
Irving Berlin

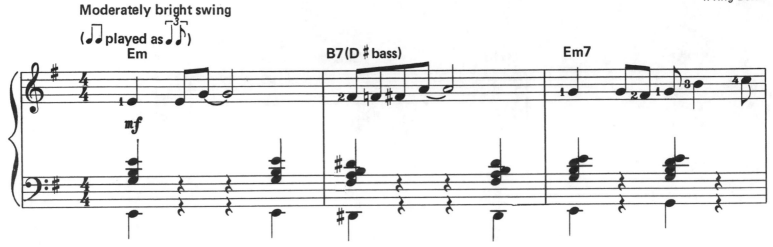

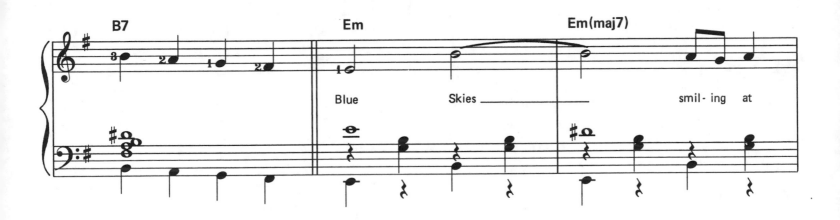

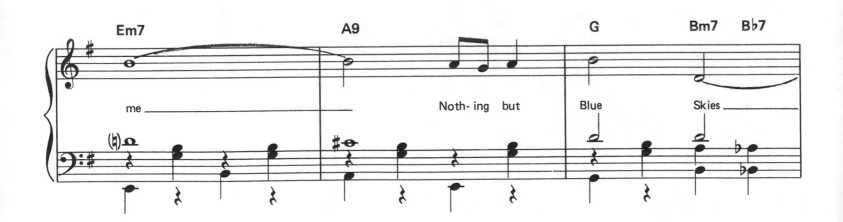

Body And Soul

Electronic and Pipe Organs

Upper: Full Organ 16', 8', 4', 2'
Lower: Diapason 8', Flutes 8', 4'
   String 4', Reed 4'
Pedal: 16', 8' Medium (Sustain)
Trem: On—Full

Drawbar Organs

Upper: 60 5585 643 (00)
Lower: (00) 7644 422 (0)
Pedal: 5 (0) 6 (0) (Spinet 5)
   String Bass
Vibrato: On—Full

Words by Edward Heyman,
Robert Sour and Frank Eyton
Music by John Green

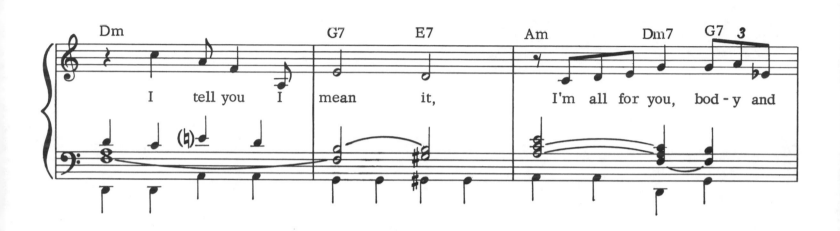

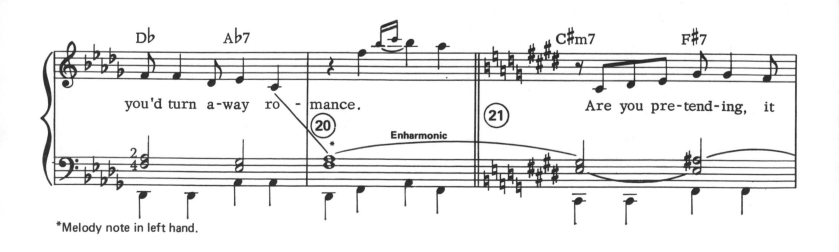

*Melody note in left hand.

looks like the end-ing Un - less I could have one more chance to prove, dear,

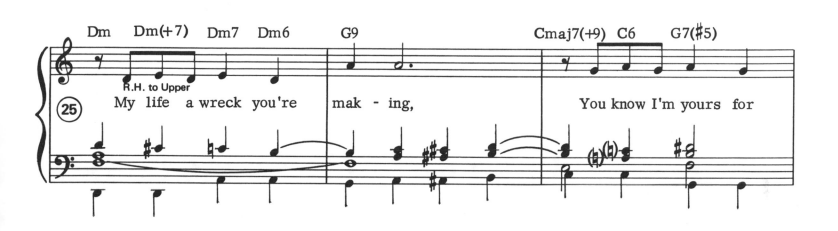

My life a wreck you're mak - ing, You know I'm yours for

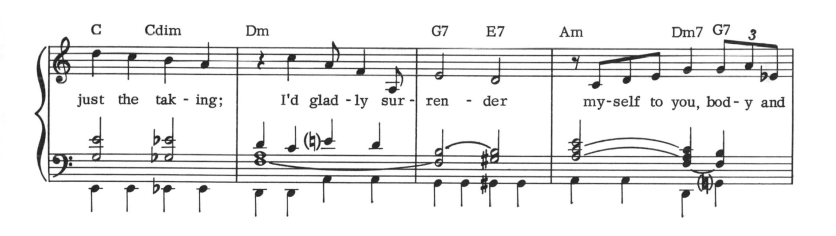

just the tak - ing; I'd glad - ly sur - ren - der my-self to you, bod - y and

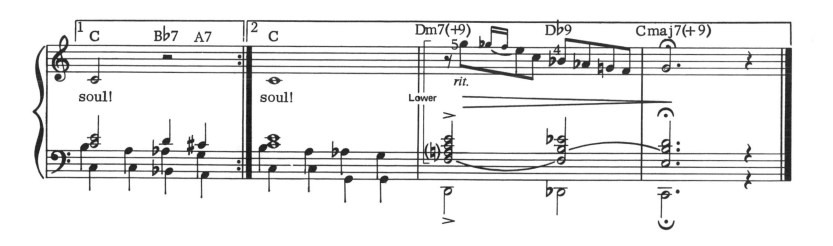

soul! soul!

Born Free
from the Columbia Pictures' Release BORN FREE

Electronic Organs
Upper: Full Organ
Lower: Full Organ
Pedal: Full Organ
Vib./Trem.: Off

Drawbar Organs
Upper: 80 0800 000
Lower: (00) 5303 000
Pedal: 24
Vib./Trem.: On, Slow

Words by Don Black
Music by John Barry

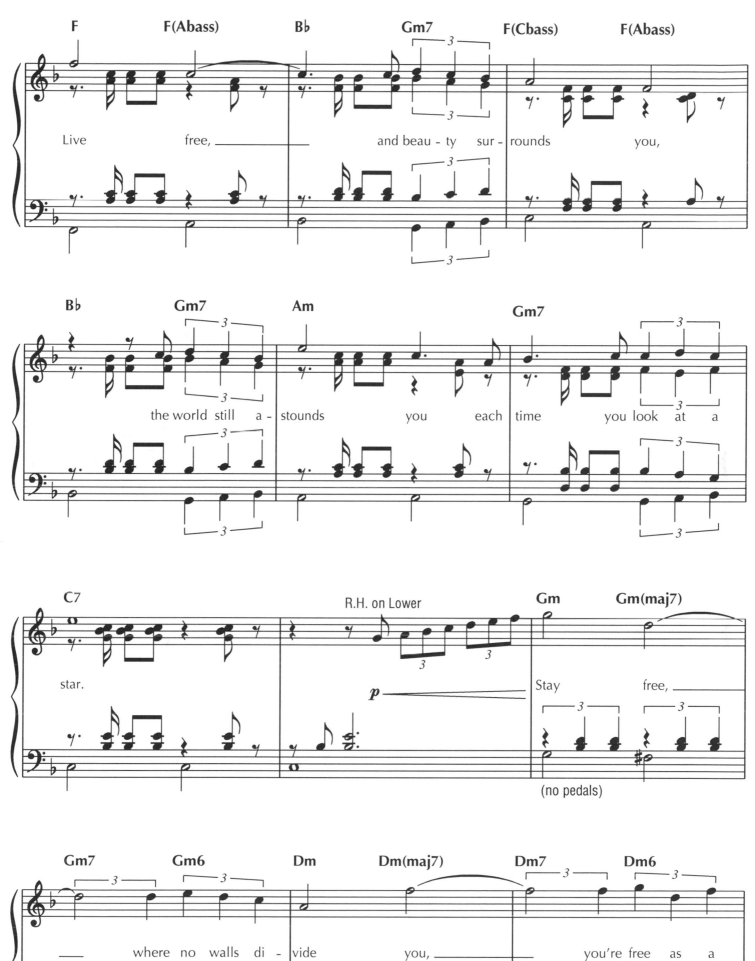

(pedals in)

roar - ing tide, so there's no need to ___ hide.

R.H. on Upper

Born free, _____ and life is worth

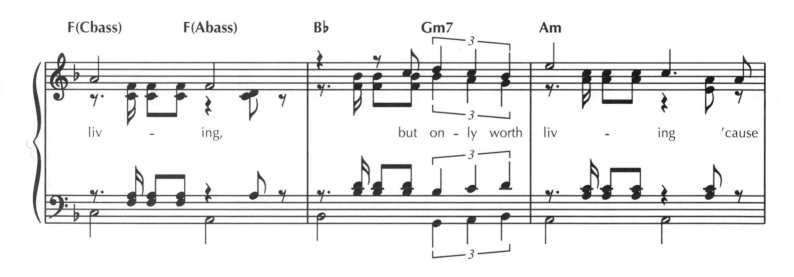

liv - ing, but on - ly worth liv - ing 'cause

you're _____ born free. _____

Call Me Irresponsible
from the Paramount Picture PAPA'S DELICATE CONDITION

Electronic Organs
Upper: 16', 8' 5 1/3 Flute
Lower: Flute 8'
Pedal: String Bass 8'
Vib./Trem.: Trem. fast

Drawbar Organs
Upper: 86 6606 000
Lower: (00) 7732 211
Pedal: 55
Vib./Trem.: On, Fast

Words by Sammy Cahn
Music by James Van Heusen

Moderately

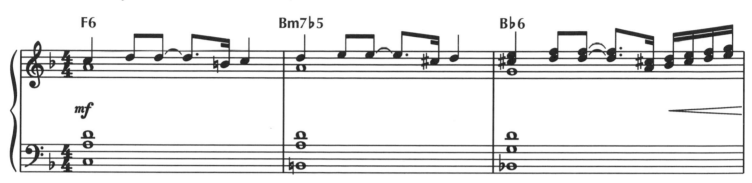

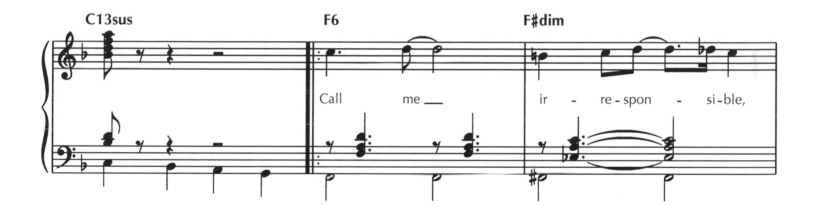

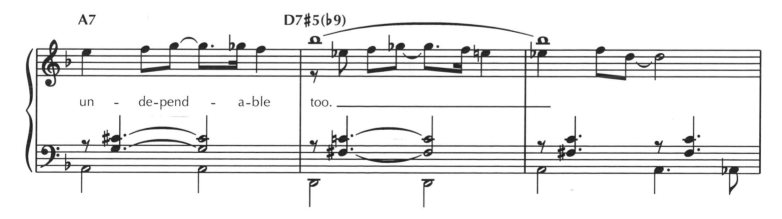

Can't Help Falling In Love

Electronic Organs
Upper: String (or Violin) 8'
Lower: Flute 8', Diapason 8'
Pedal: 16', 8' Sustain
Vib./Trem.: On, Full

Drawbar Organs
Upper: 00 5855 555
Lower: (00) 6534 211
Pedal: 53 Sustain
Vib./Trem.: On, Full

Words and Music by George David Weiss,
Hugo Peretti and Luigi Creatore

Can't Smile Without You

Electronic Organs
Upper: Flutes (or Tibias) 16', 4', Trumpet
Lower: Flute 4', Diapason 8', String 8'
Pedal: String Bass
Vib./Trem.: On, Fast

Drawbar Organs
Upper: 88 0808 088
Lower: (00) 8648 003
Pedal: String Bass
Vib./Trem.: On, Fast

Words and Music by Chris Arnold,
David Martin and Geoff Morrow

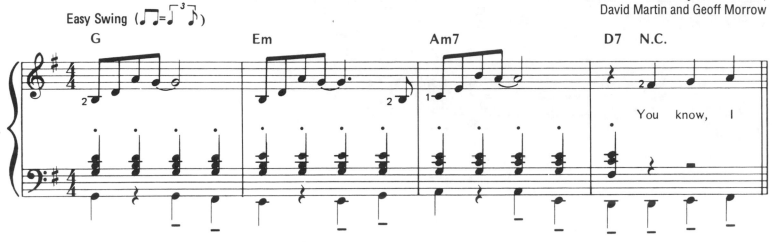

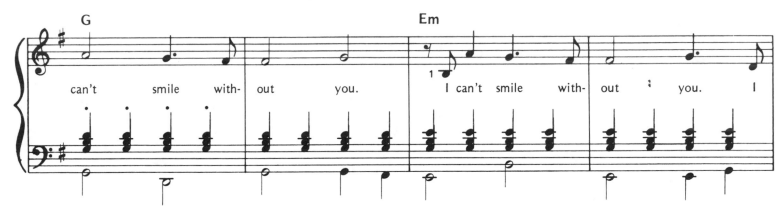

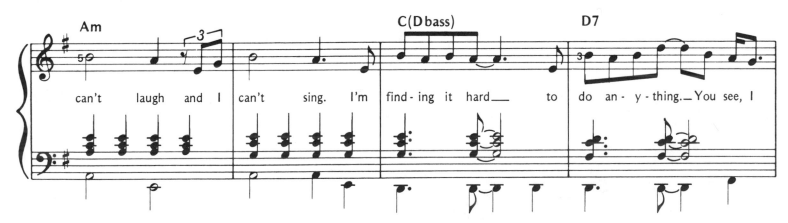

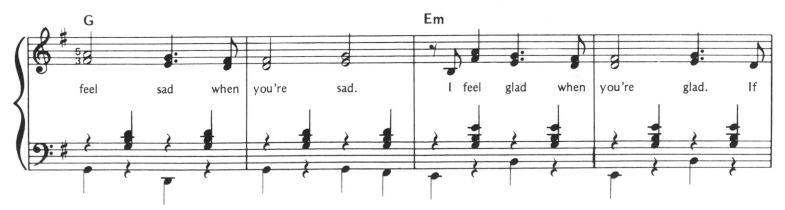

Candle In The Wind

Electronic Organs

Upper: Flutes (or Tibias) 16', 8', 4'
Lower: Melodia 8', Reed 8'
Pedal: 8'
Vib./Trem.: On, Fast

Drawbar Organs

Upper: 80 4800 000
Lower: (00) 7334 011
Pedal: 05
Vib./Trem.: On, Fast

Words and Music by Elton John
and Bernie Taupin

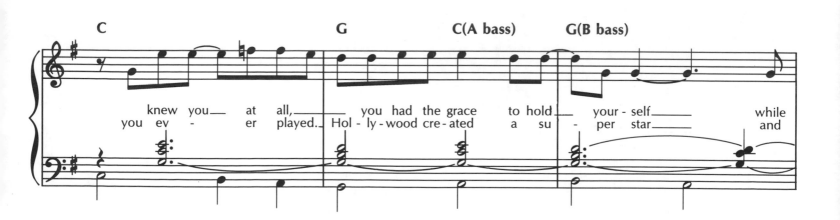

Chariots Of Fire

Electronic Organs
Upper: Synth 8' or Tpt. 8'
Lower: Fl. 8'   Reed 4'
Pedal: 16' 8'
Vib./Trem.: Slow Trem.

Drawbar Organs
Upper: 81 5355 130
Lower: (00) 8303 001
Pedal: 04
Vib./Trem.: On, Slow

Music by Vangelis

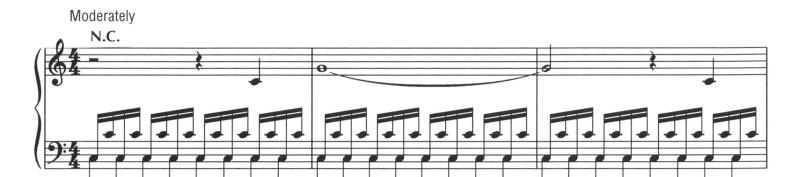

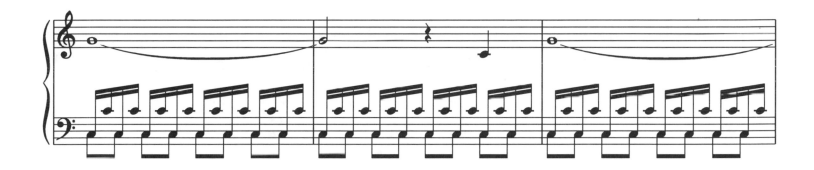

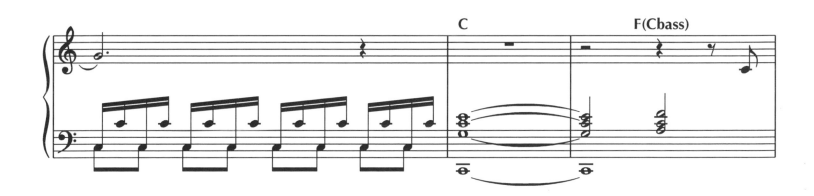

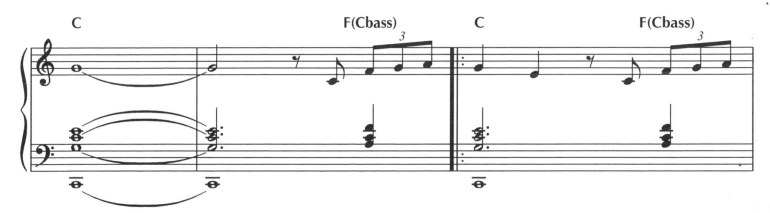

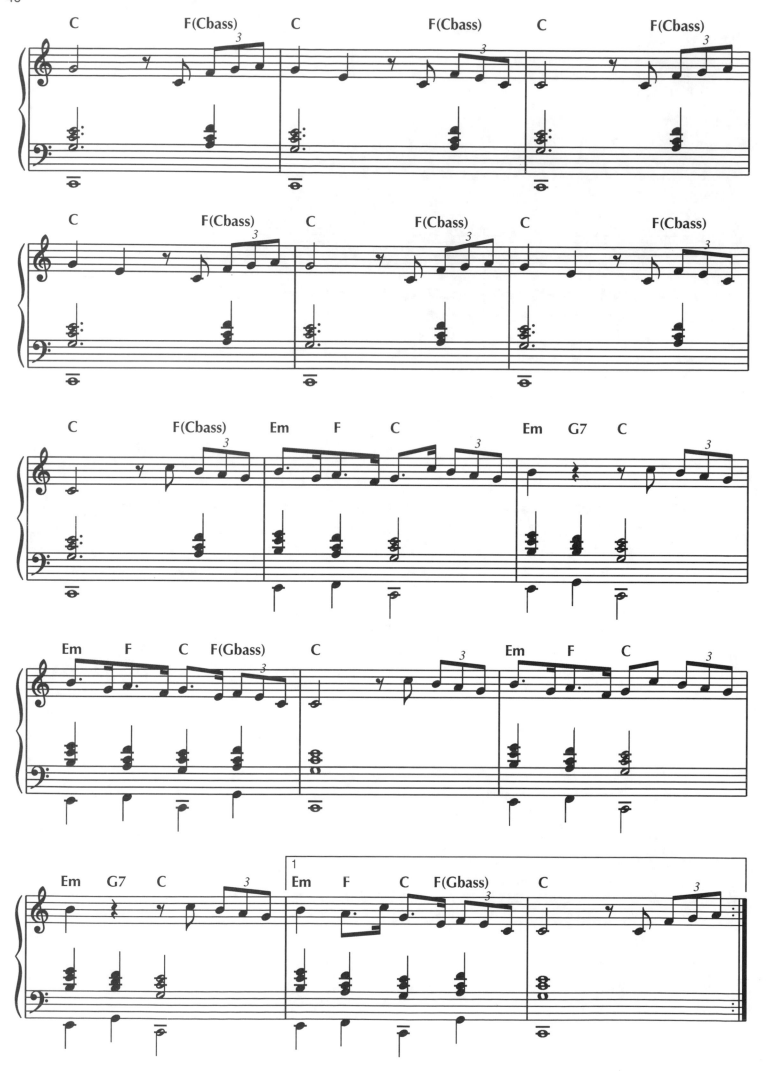

Climb Ev'ry Mountain

from THE SOUND OF MUSIC

Electronic Organs

Upper: Flute (or Tibia) 8'
Lower: Diapason 8'
Pedal: 8'
Vib./Trem.: On, Fast

Drawbar Organs

Upper: 00 8300 000
Lower: (00) 6502 000
Pedal: 04
Vib./Trem.: On, Fast

Lyrics by Oscar Hammerstein II
Music by Richard Rodgers

Crazy

Electronic Organs
Upper: Flutes (or Tibias) 16', 8', 4',
　　　　Trumpet, Oboe
Lower: Flutes 8', 4',
　　　　String 8', Reed 8'
Pedal: 16', 8'
Vib./Trem.: On, Fast

Tonebar Organs
Upper: 80 7766 008
Lower: (00) 8076 000
Pedal: 36
Vib./Trem.: On, Fast

Words and Music by
Willie Nelson

Cry Me A River

Words and Music by
Arthur Hamilton

Registration 5

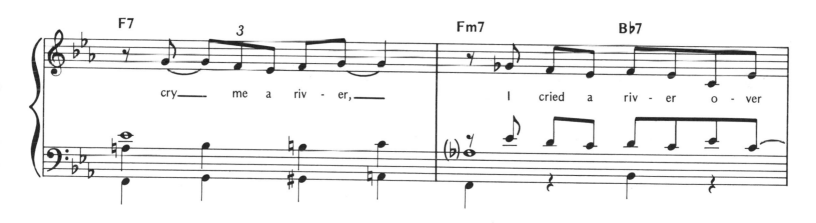

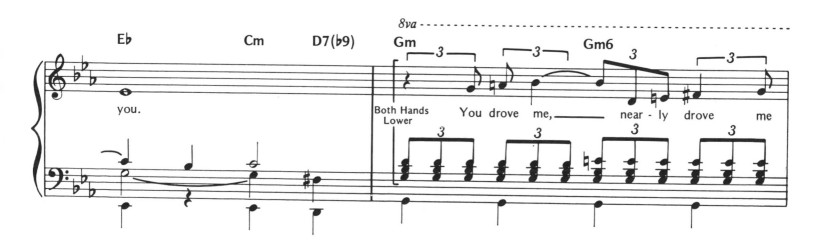

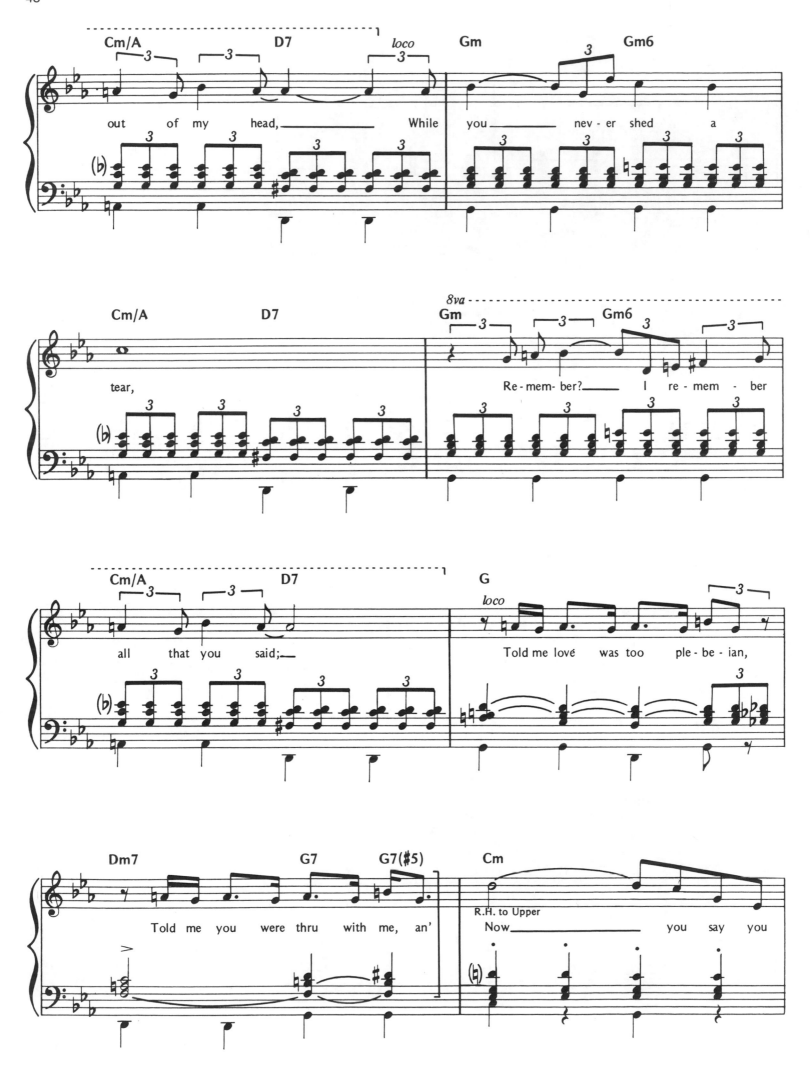

Don't Know Much

Electronic Organs

Upper: Flutes (or Tibias) 16', 4'
     Trombone
Lower: Flute 8', Melodia
Pedal: 8'
Vib./ Trem.: On, Fast

Drawbar Organs

Upper: 80 0800 000
Lower: (00) 6544 321
Pedal: 34
Vib./ Trem.: On, Fast

Words and Music by Barry Mann,
Cynthia Weil and Tom Snow

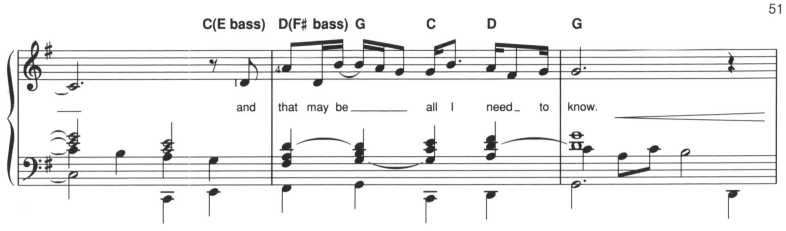

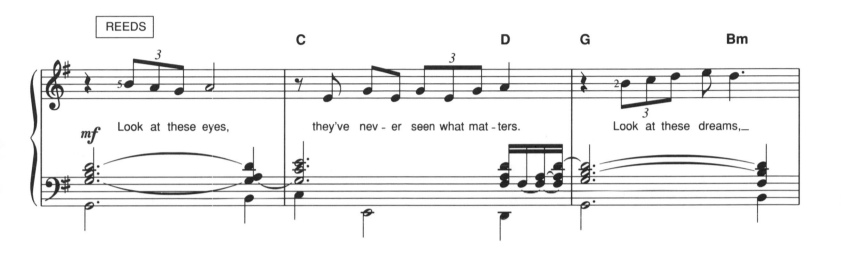

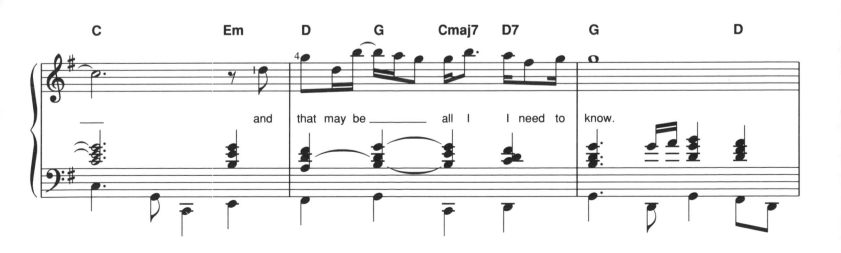

52

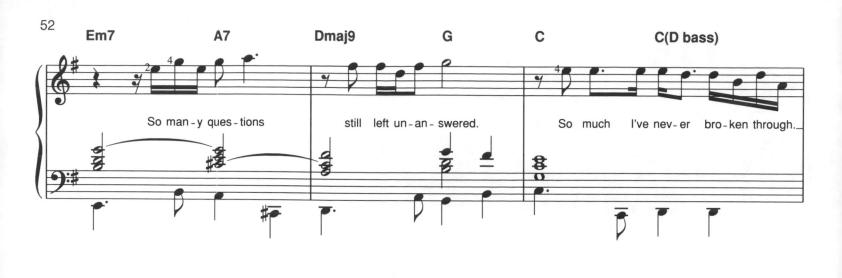

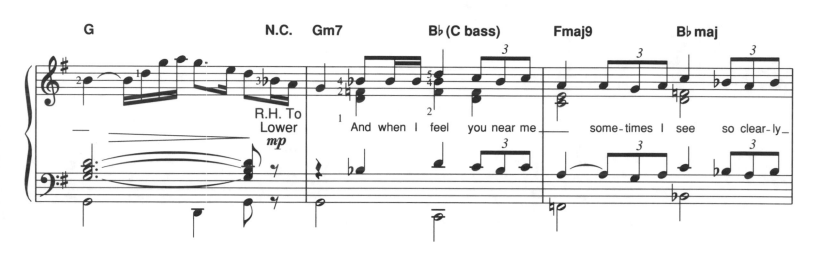

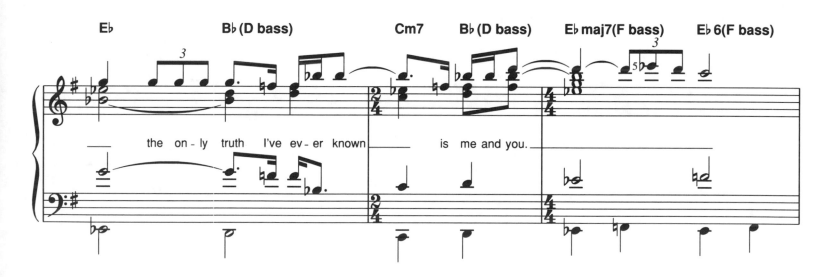

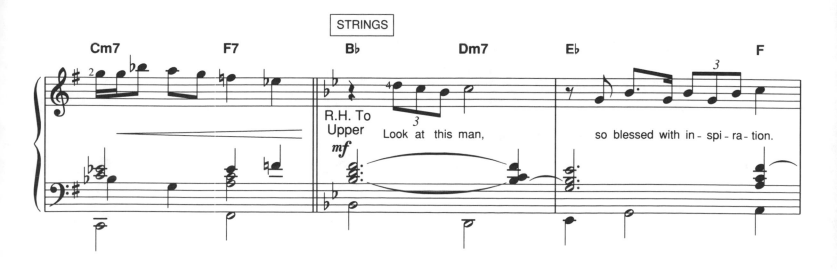

Look at this soul, _____ still search-ing for sal-va-tion. _____ I don't know _____ much,

but I know I love you, _____ and that may be _____ all I need _ to

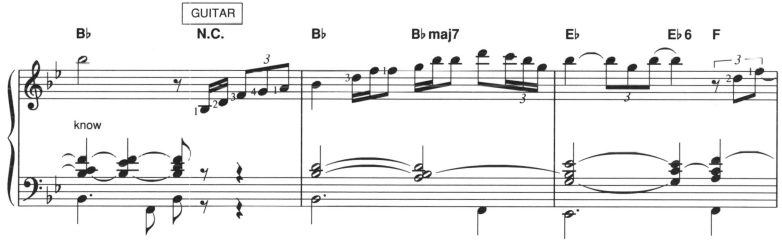

know

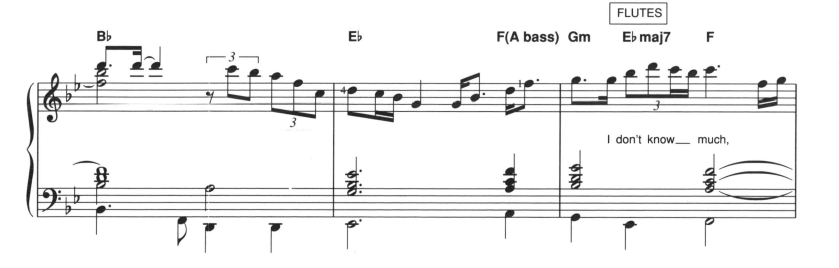

I don't know _____ much,

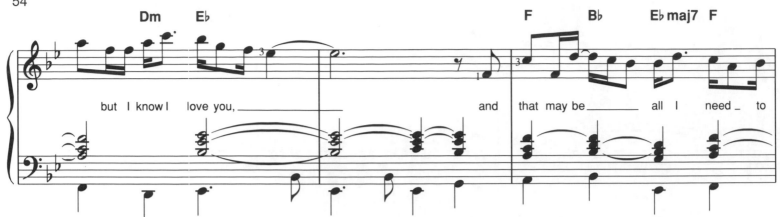

but I know I love you, _____ and that may be _____ all I need to

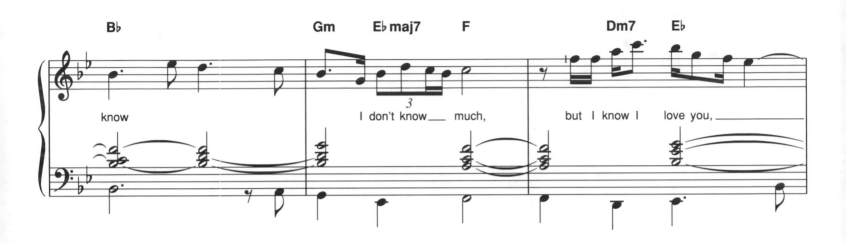

know I don't know____ much, but I know I love you, _____

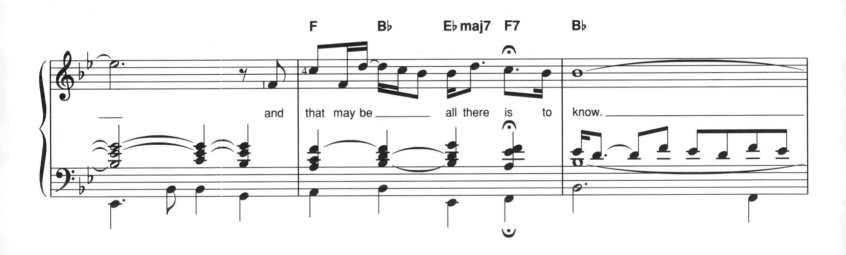

and that may be _____ all there is to know. _____

Woh. _____

The Girl From Ipanema
(Garôta De Ipanema)

Electronic Organs

Upper: Flutes (or Tibias) 16', 8', 4'
Lower: Melodia 8', Reed 8'
Pedal: 8'
Vib./Trem.: On, Fast

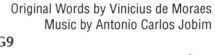

Drawbar Organs

Upper: 80 4800 000
Lower: (00) 7334 011
Pedal: 05
Vib./Trem.: On, Fast

English Words by Norman Gimbel
Original Words by Vinicius de Moraes
Music by Antonio Carlos Jobim

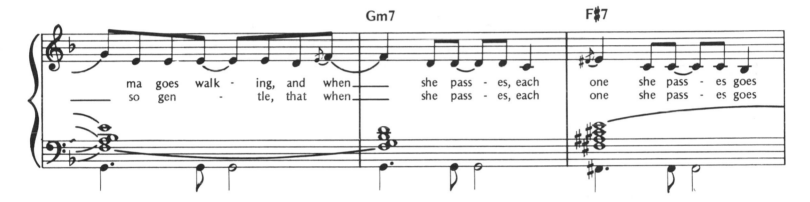

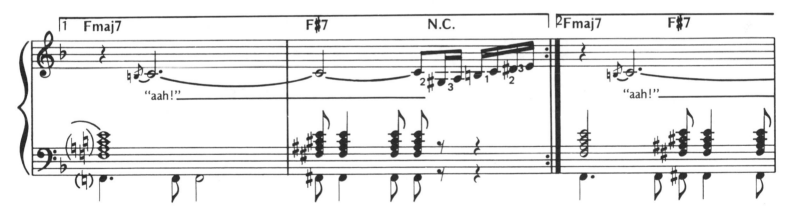

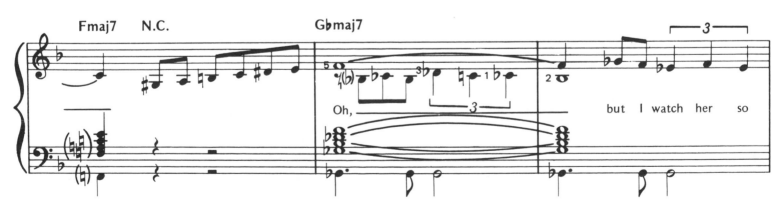

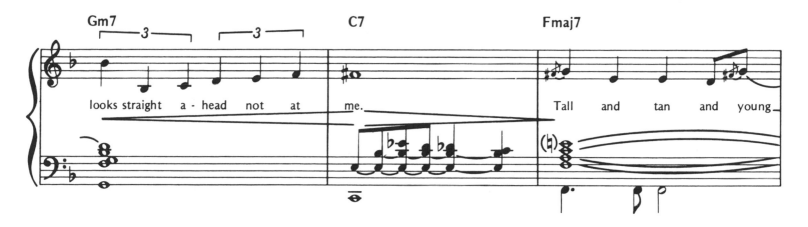

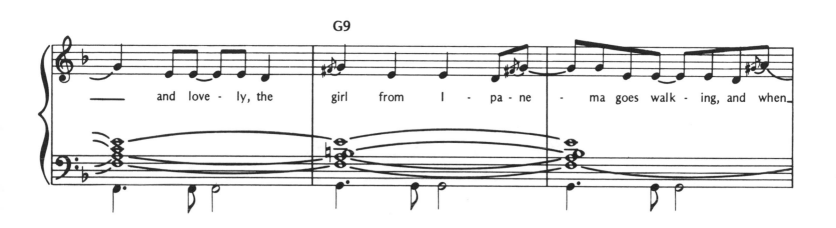

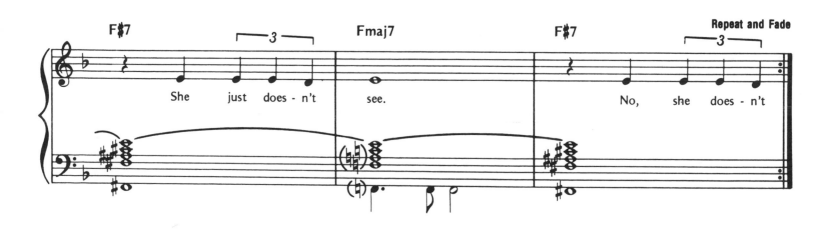

Edelweiss
from THE SOUND OF MUSIC

Electronic Organs
Upper: Flute (or Tibia) 4'
     Sustain
Lower: Flute 8'
Pedal: 8'
Vib./Trem.: On, Fast

Drawbar Organs
Upper: 00 0600 000
Lower: (00) 7000 000
Pedal: 05
Vib./Trem.: On, Fast

Lyrics by Oscar Hammerstein II
Music by Richard Rodgers

Slowly

R.H. 8va to end

Endless Love

Electronic Organs
Upper: Flutes (or Tibias) 16', 8', 4', 2',
        String 8', 4'
Lower: Flutes 8', 4',
        Strings 8', 4'
Pedal: 16', 8'
Vib./Trem.: On, Fast

Drawbar Organs
Upper: 82 5325 004
Lower: (00) 7345 312
Pedal: 44
Vib./Trem.: On, Fast

Words and Music by
Lionel Richie

Slowly - with an easy flow

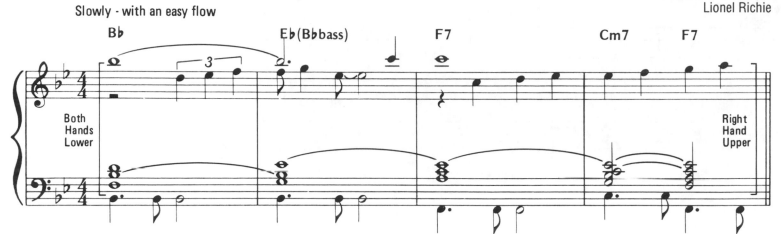

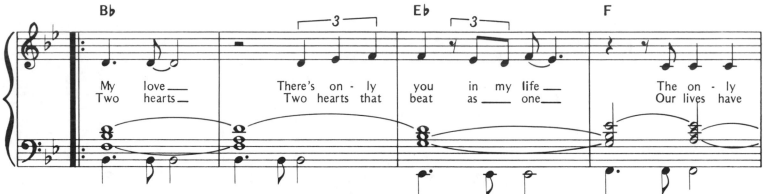

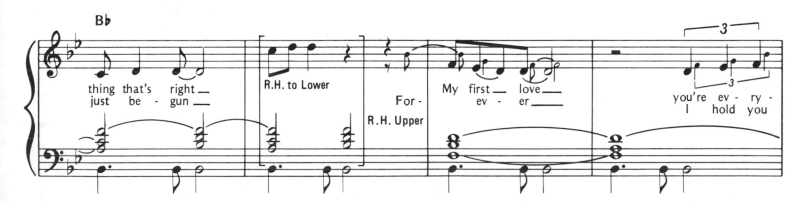

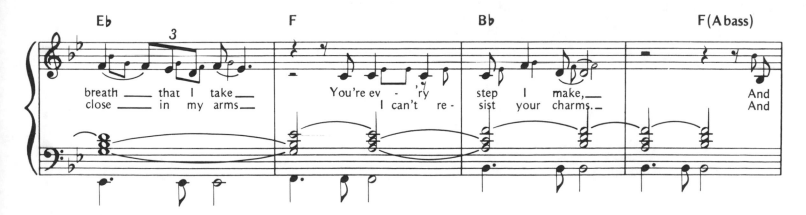

Feelings
(¿Dime?)

Electronic Organs
Upper: Flutes (or Tibias) 8', 4', 2', 1'
Lower: Flute 8', String 8'
Pedal: 16', 8', Medium
Vib./Trem.: On, Full (Opt. Off)

Drawbar Organs
Upper: 00 8282 805
Lower: (00) 6543 322
Pedal: 52
Vib./Trem.: On, Full (Opt. Off)

English Words and Music by Morris Albert
Spanish lyric by Thomas Fundora

Fly Me To The Moon
(In Other Words)

Electronic Organs
Upper: Flutes (or Tibias) 16', 2'
          Add Percussion
Lower: Flutes 8', 4'
Pedal: 16'
Vib./Trem.: On, Slow

Drawbar Organs
Upper: 80 0400 304
Lower: (00) 7404 203
Pedal: 53
Vib./Trem.: On, Slow

Words and Music by
Bart Howard

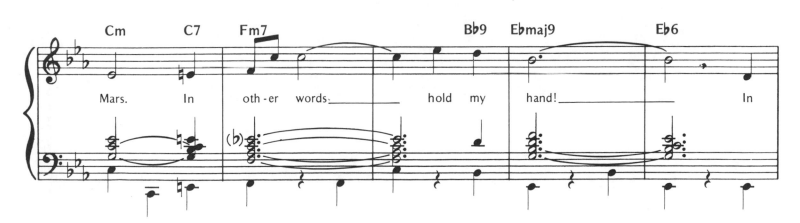

Lyrics:
Fly me to the moon, and let me play a-mong the stars; Let me see what spring is like on Ju-pi-ter and Mars. In oth-er words_____ hold my hand!_____ In

A Foggy Day
from A DAMSEL IN DISTRESS

Electronic Organs
Upper: Flutes (or Tibias) 8', 4', 2' (opt)
       Reed 8', String 4'
Lower: Flutes 8', 4', String 8' (opt)
Pedal: 16', 8'
Vib./Trem.: On, Fast

Drawbar Organs
Upper: 60 7466 003
Lower: (00) 8073 001
Pedal: 56
Vib./Trem.: On, Fast

Music and Lyrics by George Gershwin
and Ira Gershwin

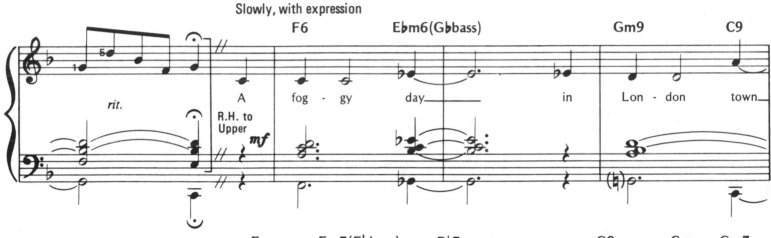

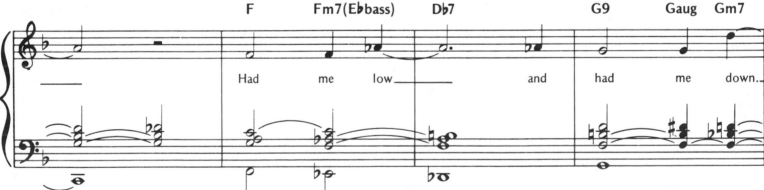

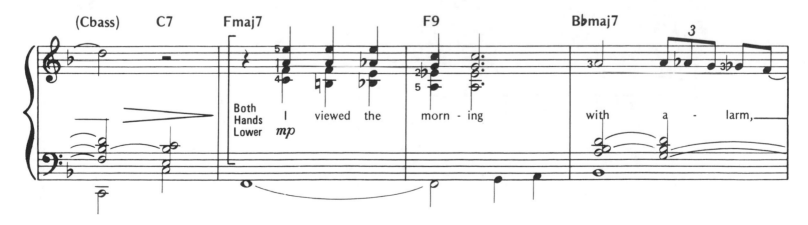

Harbor Lights

Electronic Organs

Upper:	Flutes (or Tibias) 16', 4', String 8'
Lower:	Flutes 8', 4', Diapason 8'
Pedal:	String Bass
Vib./Trem.:	On, Fast

Drawbar Organs

Upper:	60 3616 113
Lower:	(00) 7634 212
Pedal:	String Bass
Vib./Trem.:	On, Fast

Words and Music by Jimmy Kennedy
and Hugh Williams

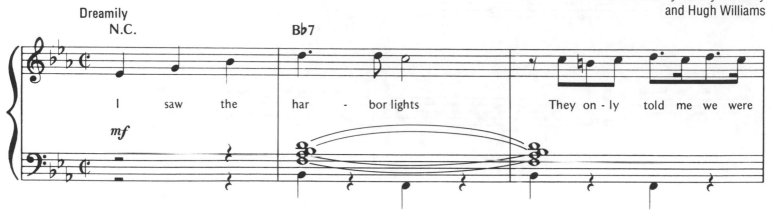

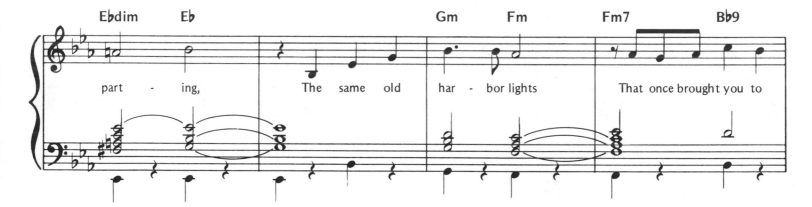

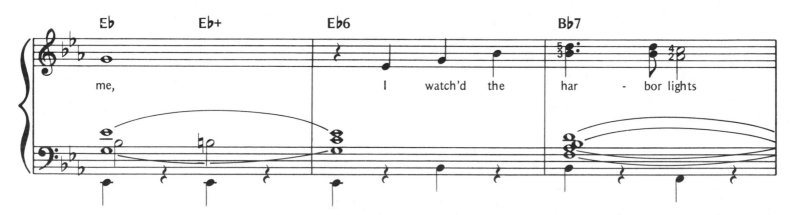

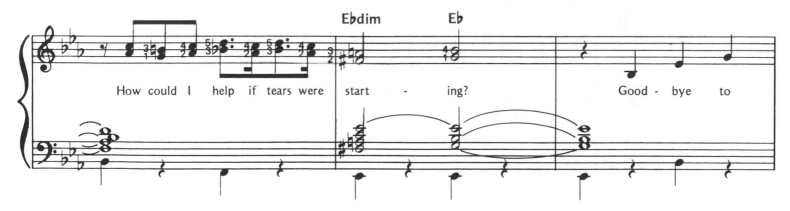

The Hawaiian Wedding Song
(Ke Kali Nei Au)

Electronic Organs
Upper: Hawaiian Guitar Preset
Lower: Flutes 8′, 4′, String 8′
Pedal: String Bass
Vib./Trem.: Vibrato On
Automatic Rhythm: Fox Trot

Drawbar Organs
Upper: Hawaiian Guitar Preset
Lower: (00) 4533 210
Pedal: 43
Vib./Trem.: Vibrato On
Automatic Rhythm: Fox Trot

English Lyrics by Al Hoffman and Dick Manning
Hawaiian Lyrics and Music by Charles E. King

Here's That Rainy Day

Electronic Organs
Upper: Flutes (or Tibias) 16', 8', 4', 2'
Lower: Flutes 8', 4', Diapason 8'
Pedal: String Bass
Vib./Trem.: On, Slow

Drawbar Organs
Upper: 80 6606 000
Lower: (00) 7400 000
Pedal: String Bass
Vib./Trem.: On, Slow

Words by Johnny Burke
Music by Jimmy Van Heusen

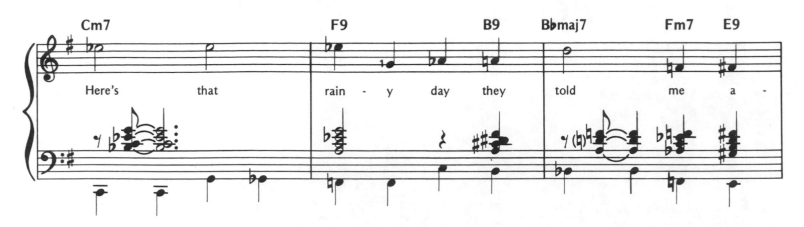

Here's that rain-y day they told me a-

bout, And I laughed at the thought that it might turn out this

way. Where is that

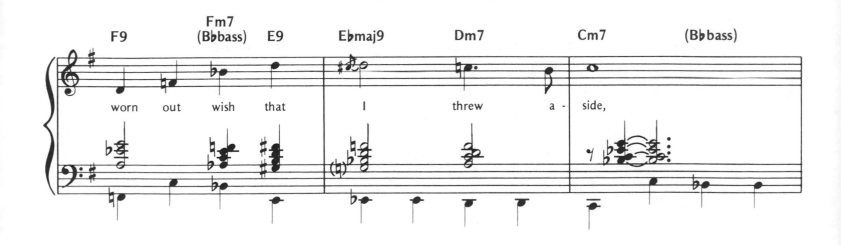

worn out wish that I threw a-side,

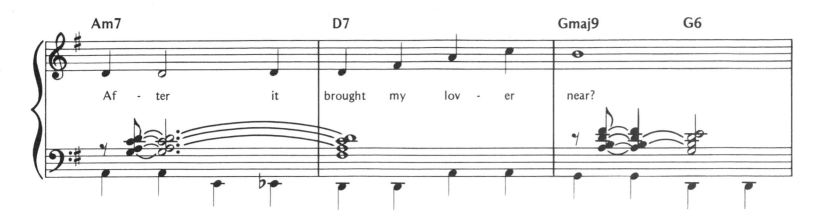

After it brought my lov-er near?

Fun - ny how love be - comes a

cold rain - y day. Fun - ny that

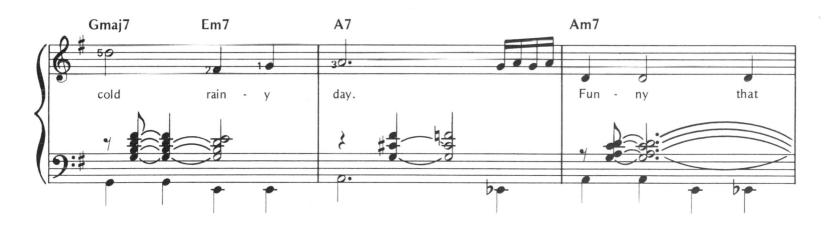

rain - y day is here.

How High The Moon
from TWO FOR THE SHOW

Electronic Organs
Upper: Flutes (or Tibias) 16′, 8′, 5⅓′, 4′, 2′
Lower: Flute 4′, Diapason 8′
Pedal: String Bass
Vib./Trem.: On, Slow

Drawbar Organs
Upper: 85 0000 355
Lower: (00) 8401 007
Pedal: String Bass
Vib./Trem.: On, Slow

Words by Nancy Hamilton
Music by Morgan Lewis

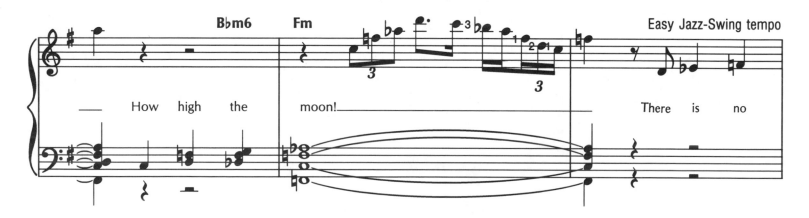

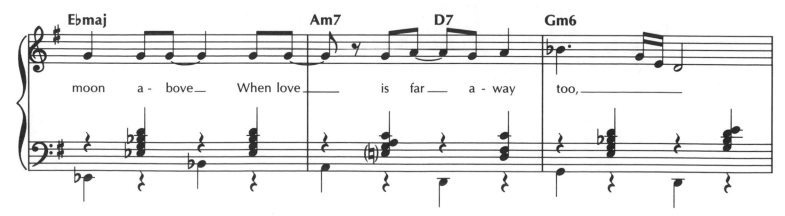

84

I Write The Songs

Electronic Organs
Upper: Piano
Lower: Strings 8', 4'
Pedal: 16', 8'
Vib./Trem.: On, Fast

Drawbar Organs
Upper: Piano
Lower: (00) 7066 000
Pedal: 34
Vib./Trem.: On, Fast

Words and Music by
Bruce Johnston

Dreamily, with expression

Lyrics:
I've ___ been a-live for-ev-er,
My home lies deep with-in you,

and I wrote the ver-y first
and I've got my own place in your

song.
soul.

I put the words and the mel-o-dies to-geth-er, I am
Now, when I look out through your eyes, I'm

mu-sic, and ___ I write the songs.
young a-gain, e-ven though I'm ver-y old.

I write the songs that make the

I Left My Heart In San Francisco

Electronic Organs
Upper: Strings 8', 4'
      Oboe
Lower: Flutes 8', 4'
Pedal: 16', 8'
Vib./Trem.: On, Fast

Drawbar Organs
Upper: 40 6502 001
Lower: (00) 6403 000
Pedal: 24
Vib./Trem.: On, Fast

Words by Douglas Cross
Music by George Cory

Slowly, with expression

Lyrics: I left my heart in San Fran- cis-co. High on a hill, it calls to me. To be where lit-tle ca-ble cars climb half-way to the stars! The morn-ing

I'll Be Seeing You

from RIGHT THIS WAY

Electronic Organs

Upper: Flutes (or Tibias) 16', 2'
Lower: Flute 8', String 8'
Pedal: String Bass
Vib./Trem: On, Fast

Drawbar Organs

Upper: 40 0006 000
Lower: (00) 4004 000
Pedal: 42
Vib./Trem.: On, Fast

Lyric by Irving Kahal
Music by Sammy Fain

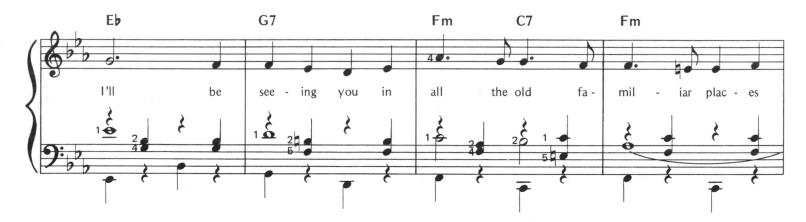

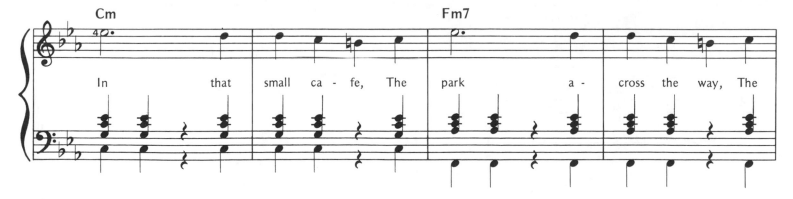

If

Electronic Organs
Upper: Solo Flute
Lower: Diapason String
Pedal: Fl.8' Gtr.8'(sust)
Vib./Trem.: Off

Drawbar Organs
Upper: 81 5505 004
Lower: (00) 7343 312
Pedal: String Bass
Vib./Trem.: Off

Words and Music by
David Gates

If a pic - ture paints a thou -
man could be two plac -

- sand words,___ then why___ can't I___ paint
- es at___ one time,___ I'd be___ with

you? The words___ will nev - er show___ the you
you, to - mor - row and to - day,___ be - side

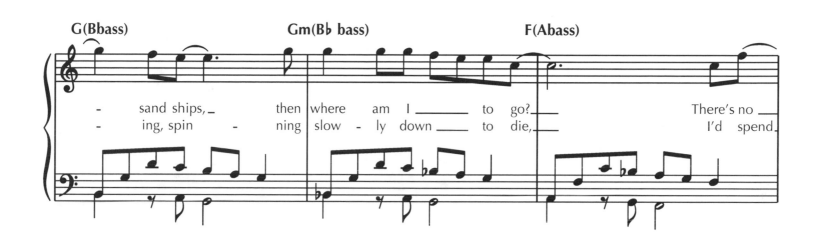

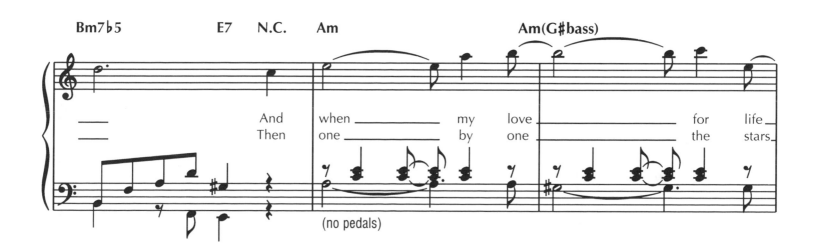

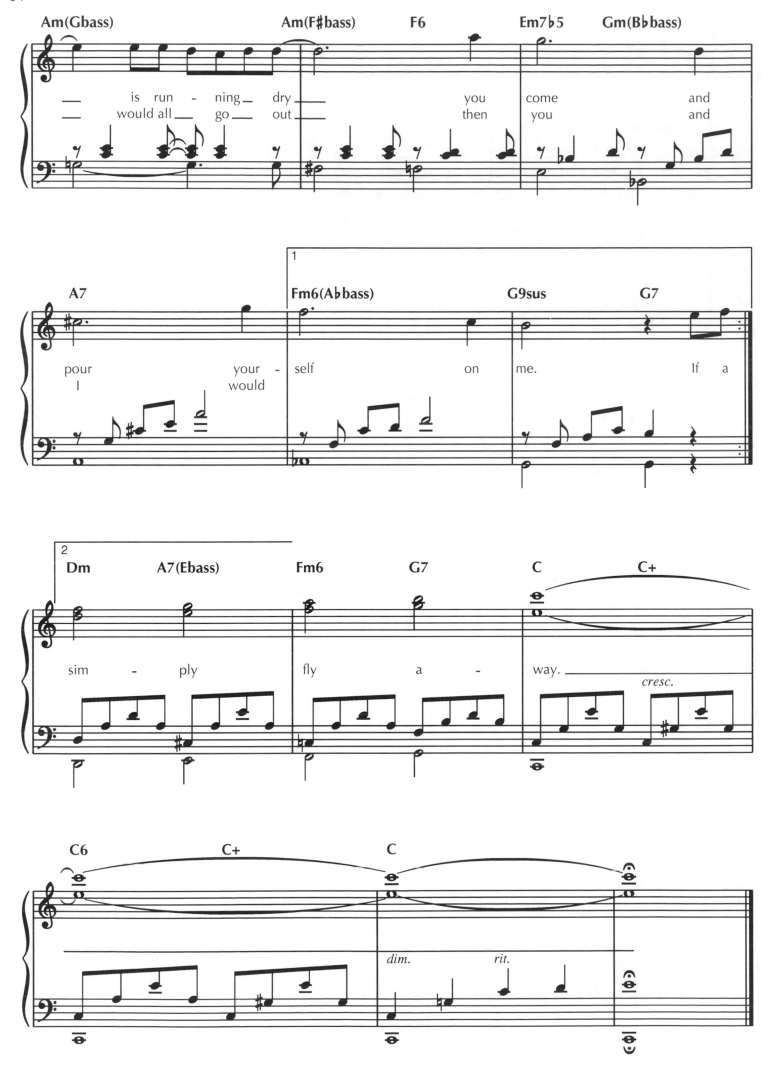

Imagine

Electronic Organs

Upper: Flutes (or Tibias) 8', 5 1/3', 4'
Lower: Strings 4', Piano
Pedal: 16', 8'
Vib./Trem.: On, Slow

Drawbar Organs

Upper: 40 0006 010
Lower: (00) 4004 000 and/or Piano
Pedal: 34
Vib./Trem.: On, Slow

Words and Music by
John Lennon

In The Mood

Electronic Organs

Upper: Flutes (or Tibias) 16', 4'
        Clarinet 8'
Lower: Flute 8', String 8'
Pedal: 16', 8'
Vib./Trem.: On, Fast

Drawbar Organs

Upper: 60 7503 002
Lower: (00) 6401 012
Pedal: 25
Vib./Trem.: On, Fast

By Joe Garland

Who's the liv-in' dol-ly with the beau-ti-ful eyes___ What a pair of lips, I'd like to
First I held her light-ly and we start-ed to dance___ Then I held her tight-ly what a

try 'em for size___ I'll just tell her, "Ba-by, won't you swing it with me"___
dream-y ro-mance___ And I said "Hey, ba-by, it's a quar-ter to three"___

Hope she tells me may-be, what a wing it will be___ So, I said po-lite-ly "Dar-lin'
There's a mess of moon-light won't-cha share it with me"___ "Well" she an-swered "Mis-ter, don't cha

may I in-trude"___ She said___ "Don't keep me wait-in' when I'm in the mood"___
know that it's rude___ To___ keep___ my two lips wait-in' when they're in the mood!"___

Fine

Isn't It Romantic?
from the Paramount Picture LOVE ME TONIGHT

Electronic Organs
Upper: Flute 16' 4', Reed 8'
Lower: Flute 4', Diap. 8'
Pedal: 16' 8'
Vib./Trem.: OFF until Chorus

Drawbar Organs
Upper: 80 7003 051
Lower: (00) 7303 004
Pedal: String Bass
Vib./Trem.: On, Slow

Words by Lorenz Hart
Music by Richard Rodgers

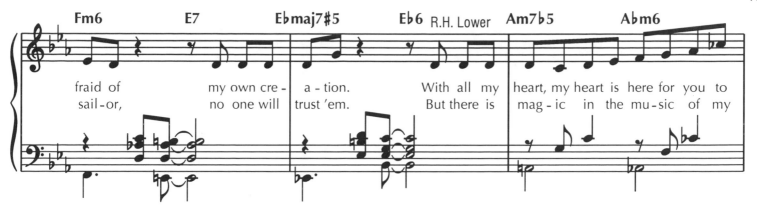

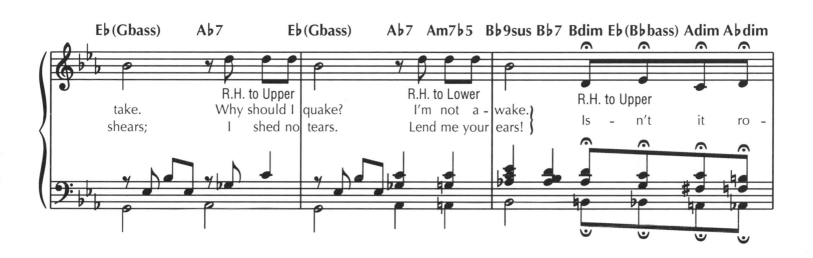

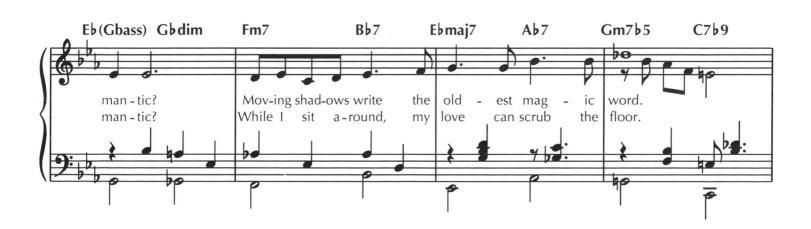

I hear the breez-es play - ing in the trees a -
She'll kiss me ev -'ry hour,____ or she'll get the

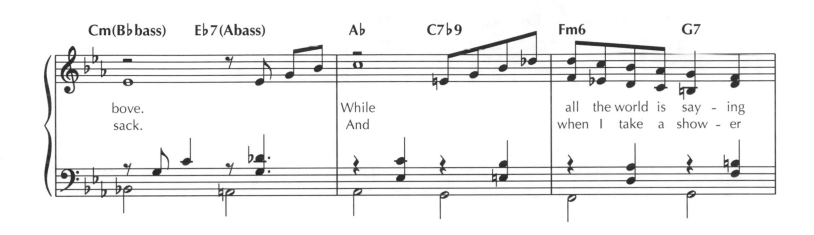

bove. While all the world is say - ing
sack. And when I take a show - er

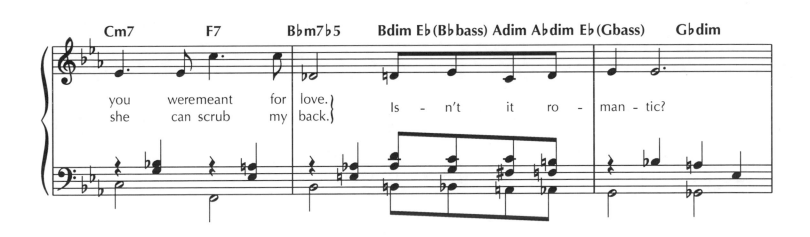

you were meant for love.} Is - n't it ro - man - tic?
she can scrub my back.}

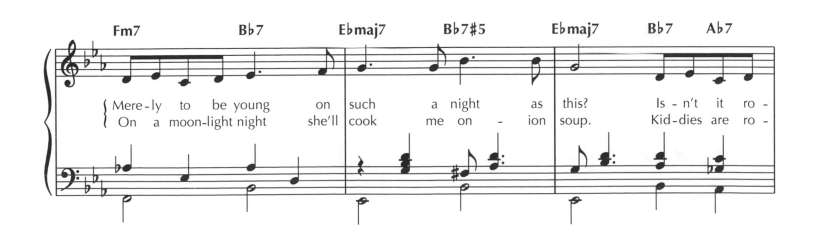

Mere-ly to be young on such a night as this? Is - n't it ro -
On a moon-light night she'll cook me on - ion soup. Kid-dies are ro -

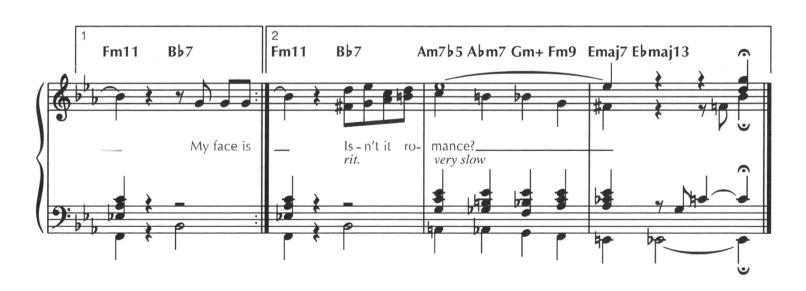

Just The Way You Are

Electronic Organs
Upper: Flutes (or Tibias) 16′, 8′, 5⅓′, 4′, 2′
Lower: Flutes 8′, 4′, Diapason 8′,
    Reed 8′
Pedal: 16′, 8′
Vib./Trem.: On, Fast

Drawbar Organs
Upper: 86 6606 000
Lower: (00) 7732 211
Pedal: 55
Vib./Trem.: On, Fast

Words and Music by
Billy Joel

Just In Time
from BELLS ARE RINGING

Electronic Organs
Upper: Flutes (or Tibias) 16′, 8′ 5⅓′,
          4′, 2′
Lower: Flutes 8′, 4′, Diapason 8′, Reed 8′
Pedal: 16′, 8′
Vib./Trem.: On, Fast

Drawbar Organs
Upper: 86 6606 000
Lower: (00) 8832 211
Pedal: 55
Vib./Trem.: On, Fast

Words by Betty Comden and Adolph Green
Music by Jule Styne

Moderately

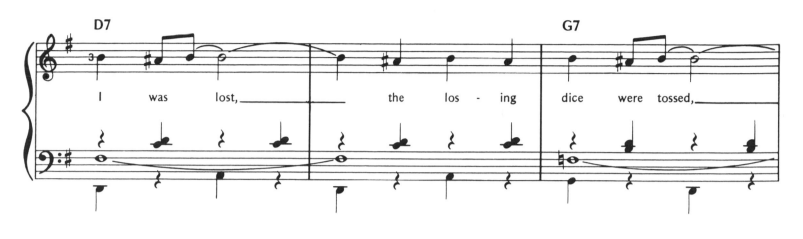

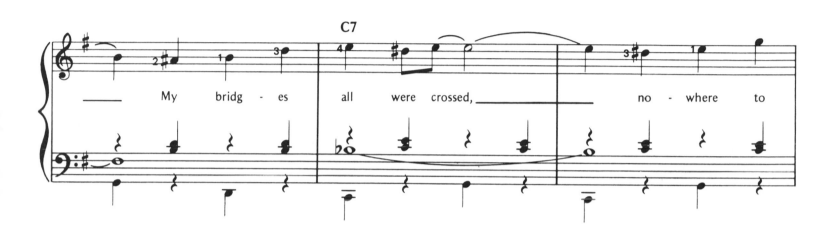

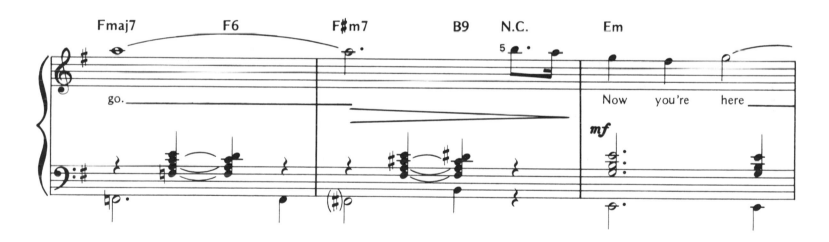

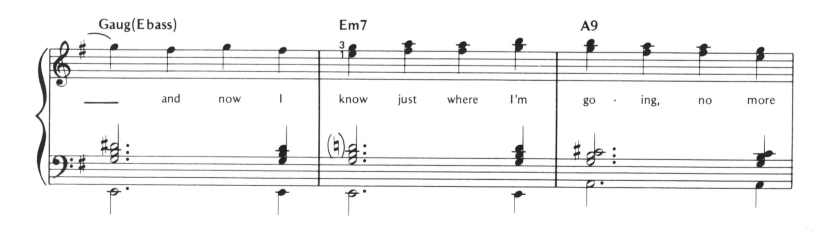

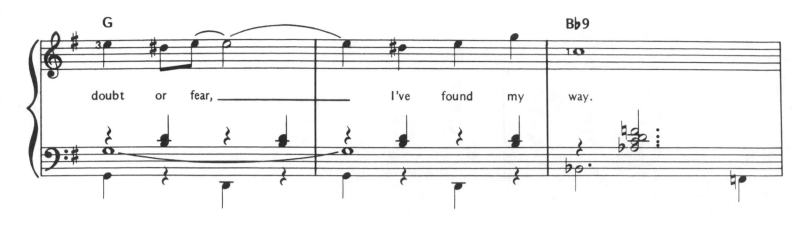

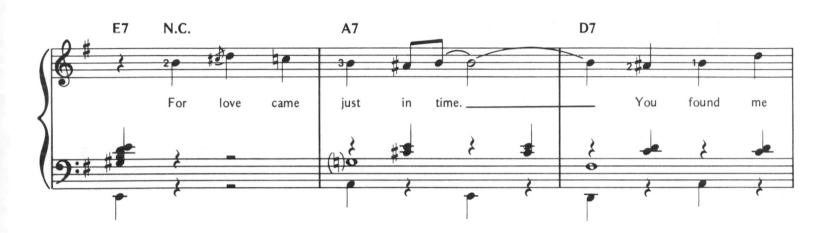

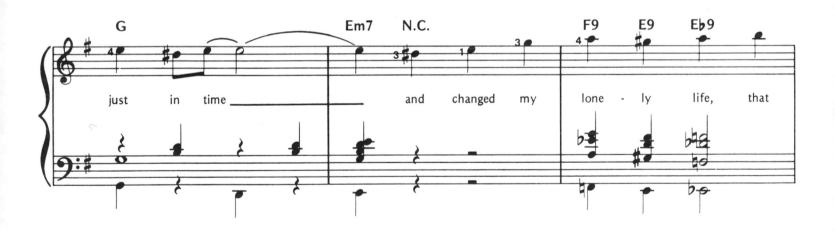

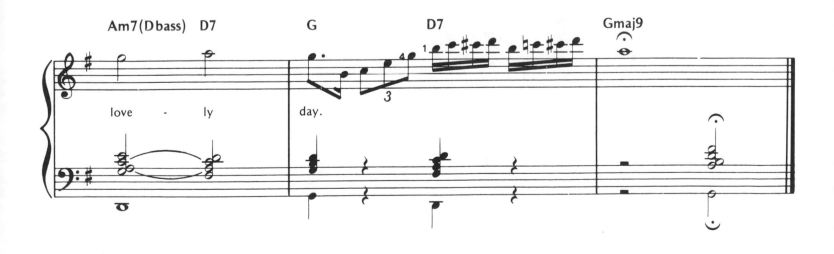

Let It Be

Electronic Organs
Upper: Flutes (or Tibias) 16', 8', 4'
Lower: Melodia 8', Reed 8'
Pedal: 8'
Vib./Trem.: On, Fast

Tonebar Organs
Upper: 80 4800 000
Lower: (00) 7334 011
Pedal: 05
Vib./Trem.: On, Fast

Words and Music by John Lennon
and Paul McCartney

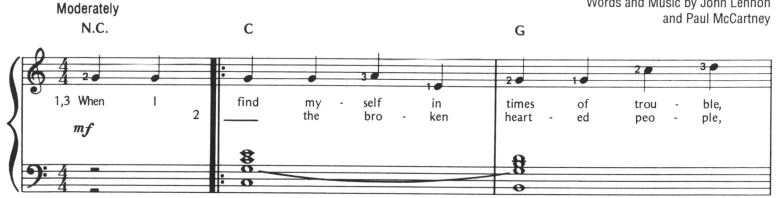

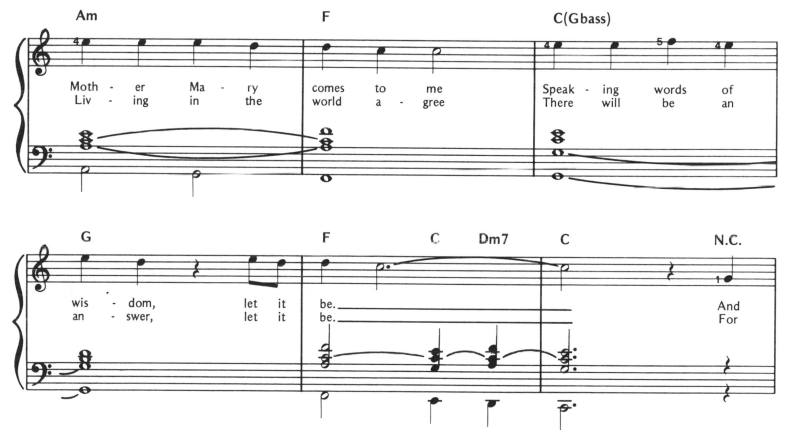

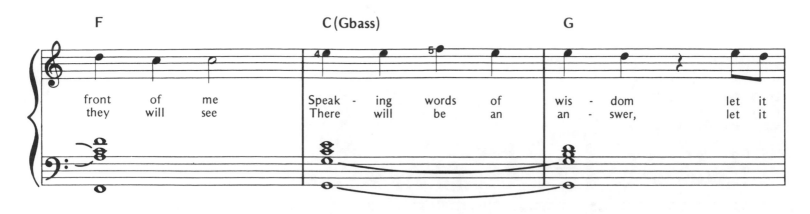

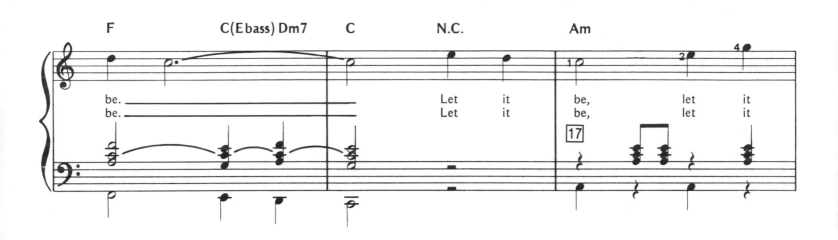

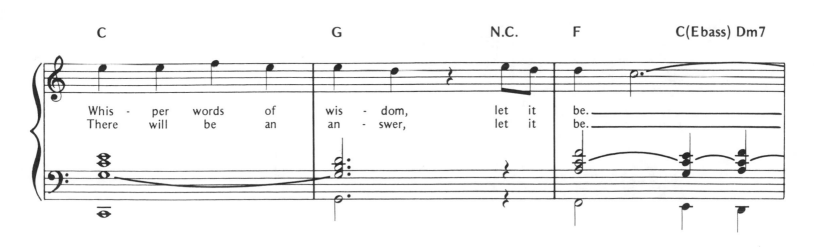

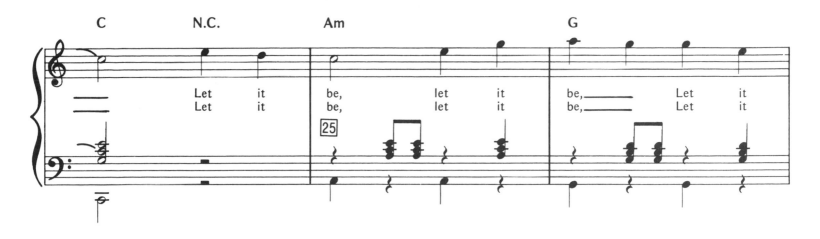

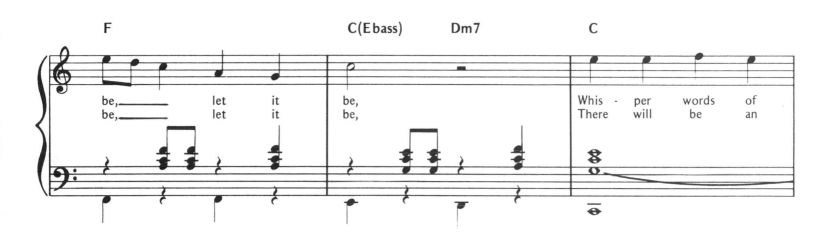

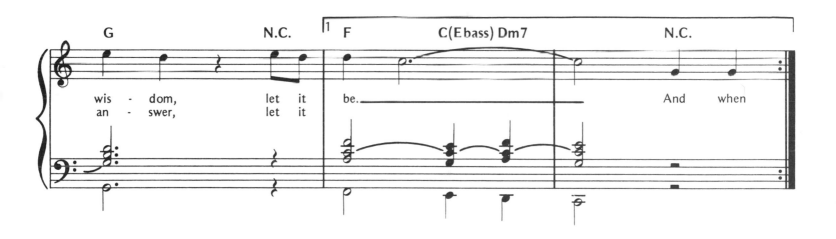

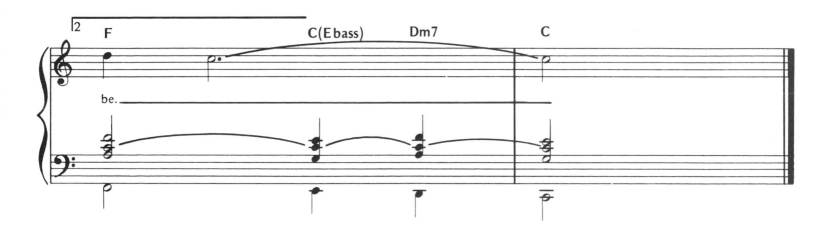

The Lady Is A Tramp

Electronic Organs
Upper: Flutes (or Tibias) 16', 8', 4'
   Trumpet, Oboe
Lower: Flutes 8', 4', Diapason 8',
   Reed 8'
Pedal: 16', 8'
Vib./Trem.: On, Fast

Drawbar Organs
Upper: 80 7766 008
Lower: (00) 8076 000
Pedal: 36
Vib./Trem.: On, Fast

Words by Lorenz Hart
Music by Richard Rodgers

Lyrics:

I get too hun-gry for din-ner at eight, I like the thea-tre but nev-er come late. I nev-er

Longer

Electronic Organs

Upper: Trumpet
Lower: Strings 8', 4'
Pedal: 16', 8'
Vib./Trem.: On, Fast

Drawbar Organs

Upper: 70 6365 005
Lower: (00) 8376 000
Pedal: 45
Vib./Trem.: On, Fast

Words and Music by
Dan Fogelberg

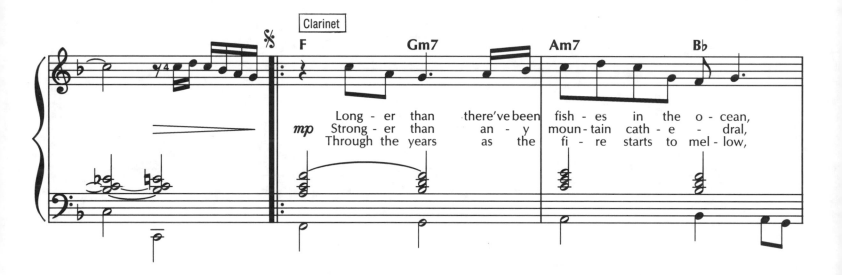

Long - er than there've been fish - es in the o - cean,
Strong - er than an - y moun - tain cath - e - dral,
Through the years as the fi - re starts to mel - low,

high - er than an - y bird ev - er flew,—
tru - er than an - y tree ev - er grew,—
burn - ing lines in the book of our lives.—

Long - er than there've been
Deep - er than an - y
Though the bind - ing cracks— and the

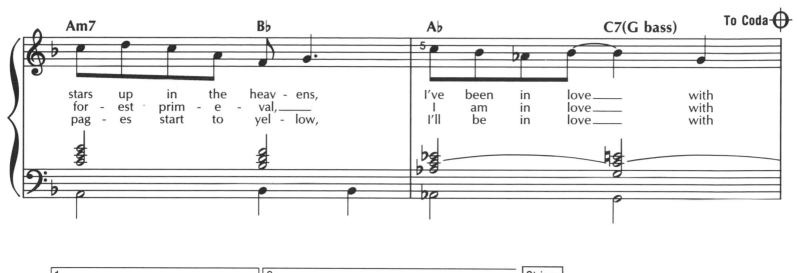

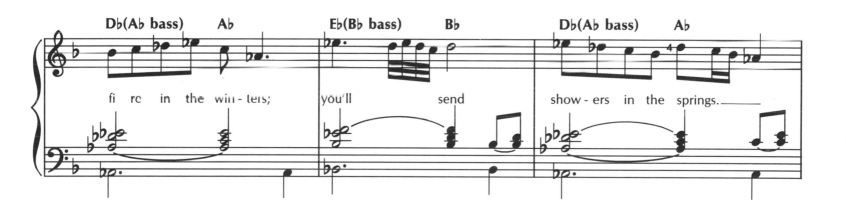

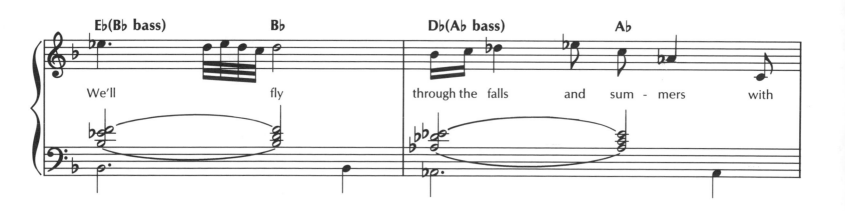

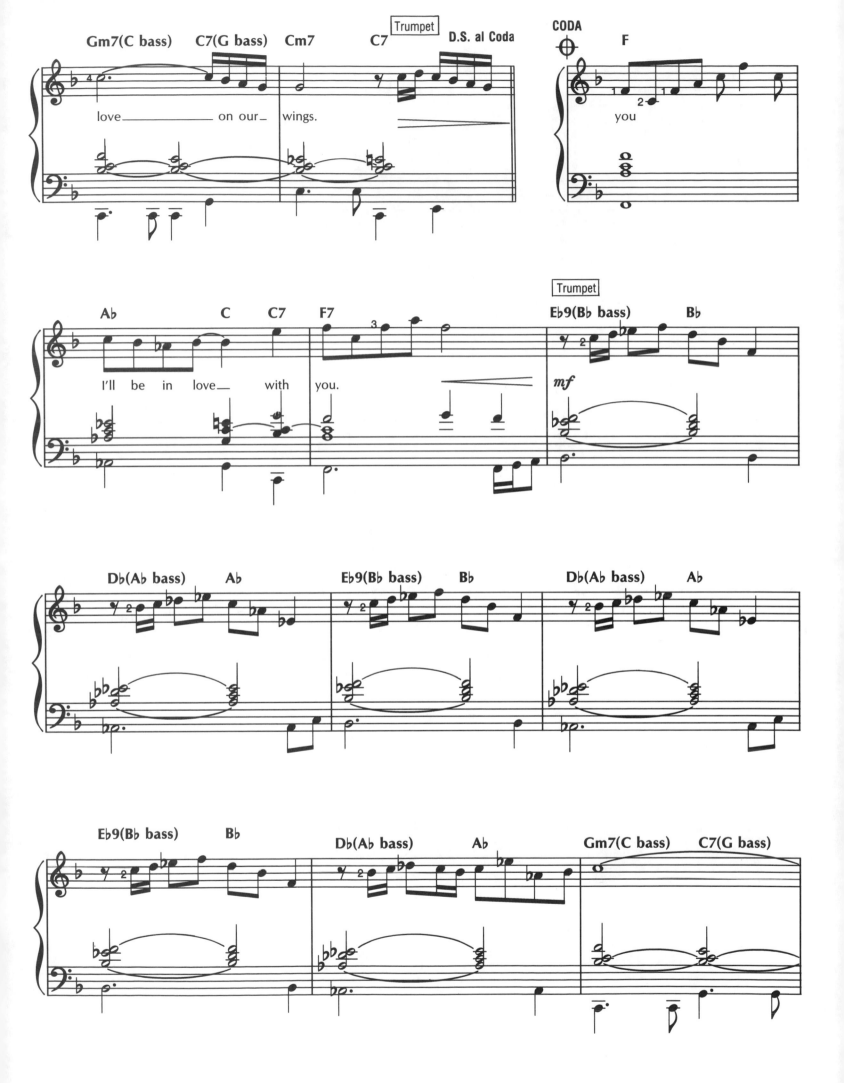

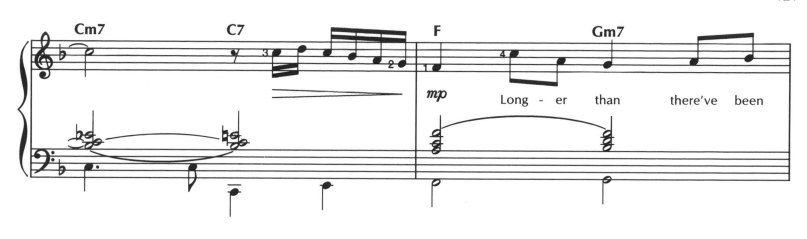

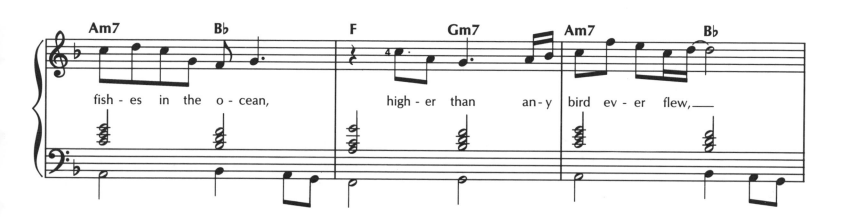

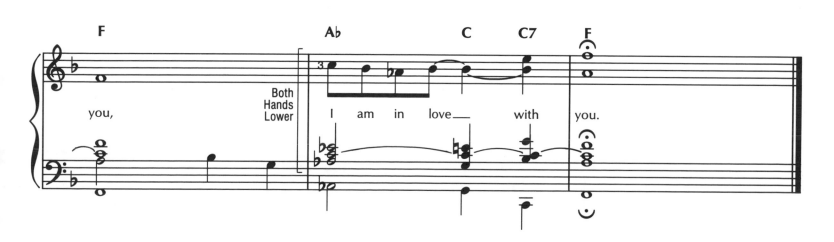

Love Is Blue
(L'amour Est Bleu)

Electronic Organs

Upper: Flutes (or Tibias) 16', 4', 2'
Lower: Flutes 8', 4'
Pedal: 8'
Vib./Trem.: On, Fast

Drawbar Organs

Upper: 80 0402 304
Lower: (00) 7404 203
Pedal: 34
Vib./Trem.: On, Fast

English Lyric by Brian Blackburn
Original French Lyric by Pierre Cour
Music by Andre Popp

Love Me Tender

Electronic Organs
Upper: Flute (or Tibia) 16',
       Clarinet 8'
Lower: Flutes 8', 4', String 4'
Pedal: 16', 8' Sustain
Vib./Trem.: On Full

Drawbar Organs
Upper: 60 8080 806
Lower: (00) 7654 321
Pedal: 55 Sustain
Vib./Trem.: On, Full

Words and Music by Elvis Presley
and Vera Matson

Slowly, with expression

mp

rit.

G   F#   G(F bass)   A7   (E♭ bass)

Love me ten - der, love me sweet;
Love me ten - der, love me long;

mp (a tempo)

D7   G   F#   G(F bass)

Nev - er let me go. You have made my
Take me to your heart. For it's made there that

A7   (E♭ bass)   D7   G

life com - plete, And I love you so. }
I be - long, And we'll nev - er part. }

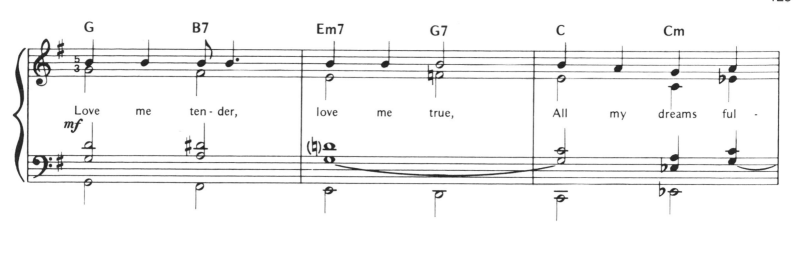

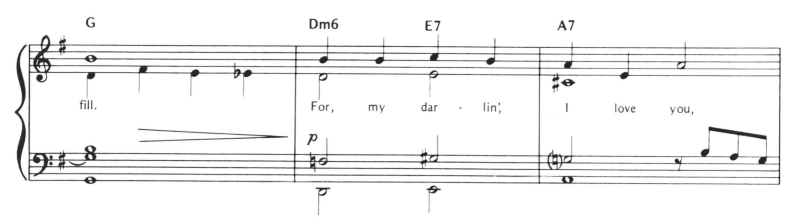

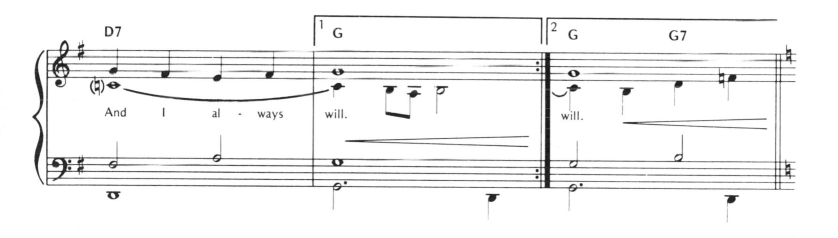

Moon River
from the Paramount Picture BREAKFAST AT TIFFANY'S

Electronic Organs
Upper: Tromb. Flute 4'
Lower: Clar., Flute 4' (or string ensemble)
Pedal: String Bass 8'
Vib./Trem.: Slow

Drawbar Organs
Upper: 80 6606 000
Lower: (00) 7400 000
Pedal: String Bass
Vib./Trem.: On, Slow

Words by Johnny Mercer
Music by Henry Mancini

Memory
from CATS

Electronic Organs
Upper: Flutes (or Tibias) 8', 4', 2'
        Strings 8'
        Clarinet
Lower: Flutes 8', 4'
Ped.: 16', 8'
Vib./Trem.: On, Slow

Drawbar Organs
Upper: 30 8104 103
Lower: (00) 6303 004
Ped.:   25
Vib./Trem.: On, Slow

Music by Andrew Lloyd Webber
Text by Trevor Nunn
after T.S. Eliot

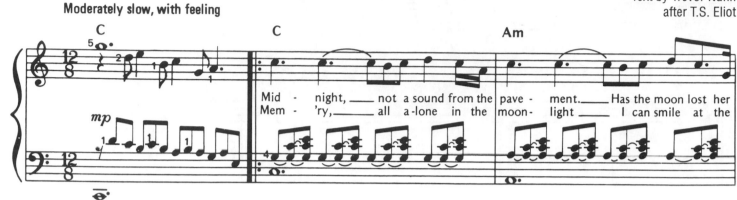

Moderately slow, with feeling

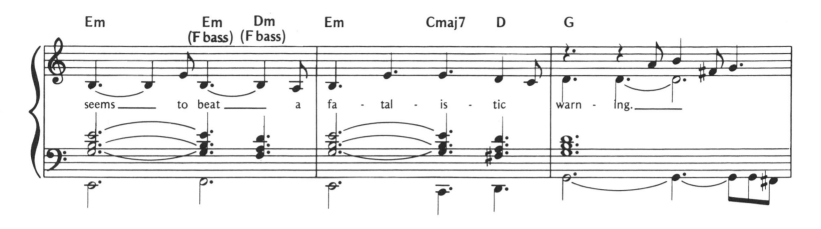

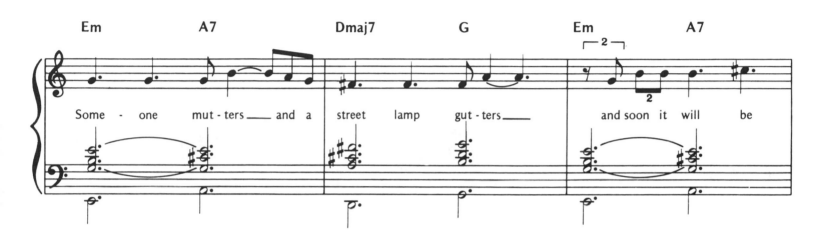

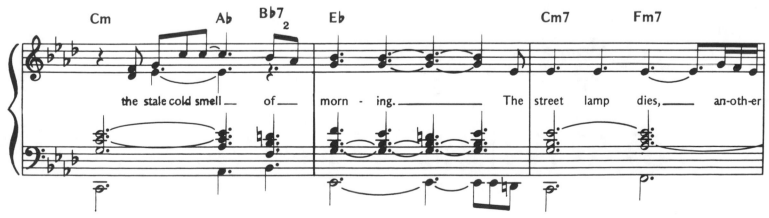

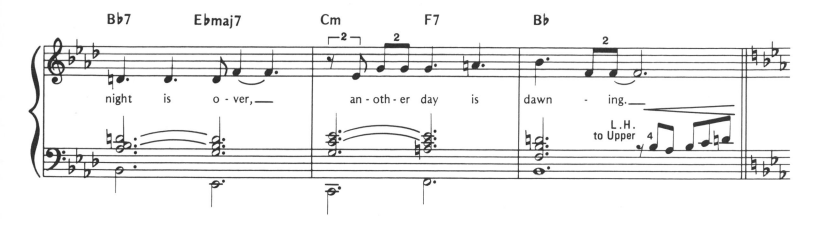

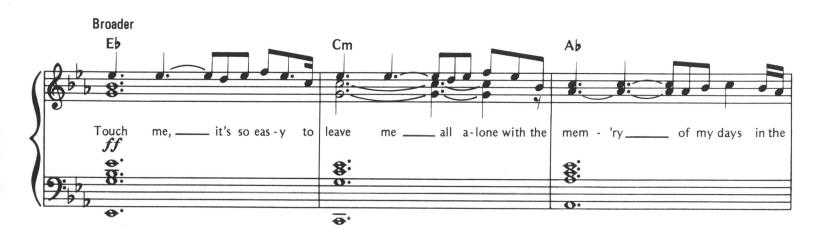

Moonglow

Electronic Organs
Upper: Flutes (or Tibias) 16', 8',
          5⅓', 4', 2'
Lower: Flute 8', 4'
        Diapason 8', Reed 8'
Pedal: 16', 8'
Vib./Trem: On, Fast

Drawbar Organs
Upper 86 6606 000
Lower: (00) 7732 211
Pedal: 55
Vib./Trem.: On, Fast

Words and Music by Will Hudson,
Eddie De Lange and Irving Mills

My Favorite Things
from THE SOUND OF MUSIC

Electronic Organs

Upper: Flutes (or Tibias) 16', 4',
      String 8'
Lower: Flutes 8', 4', Diapason 8'
Pedal: String Bass
Vib./Trem.: On, Fast

Drawbar Organs

Upper: 60 3613 113
Lower: (00) 7634 212
Pedal: String Bass
Vib./Trem.: On, Fast

Lyrics by Oscar Hammerstein II
Music by Richard Rodgers

Brightly

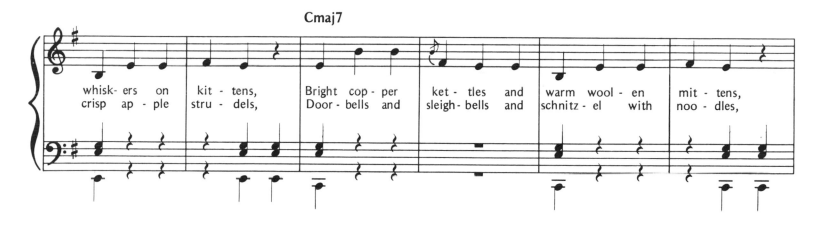

138

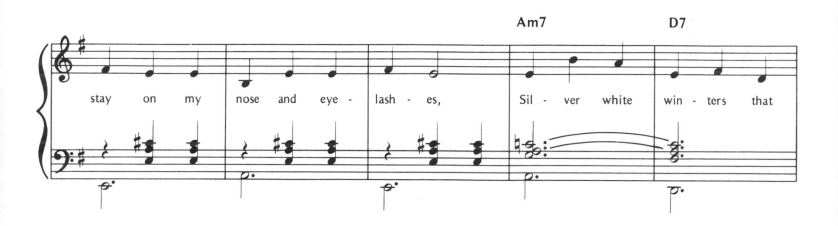

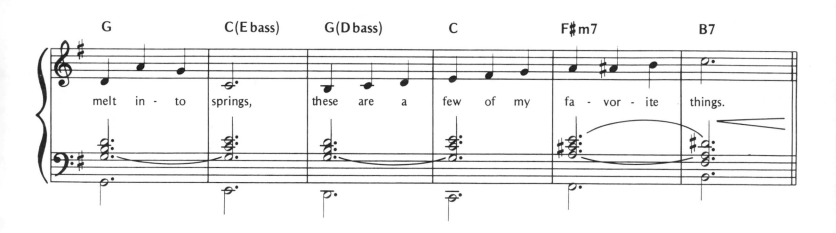

feel - ing sad,   simply re - mem - ber my

loco L.H. to Lower

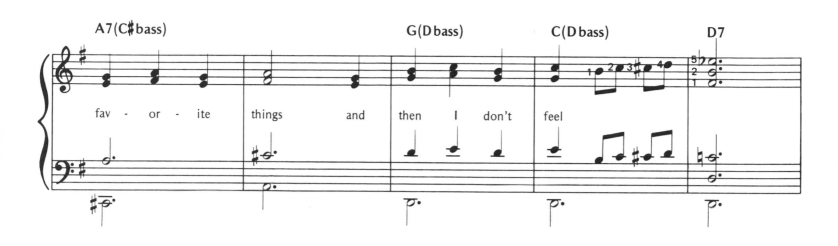

A7(C#bass)   G(Dbass)   C(Dbass)   D7

fav - or - ite   things   and   then   I   don't   feel

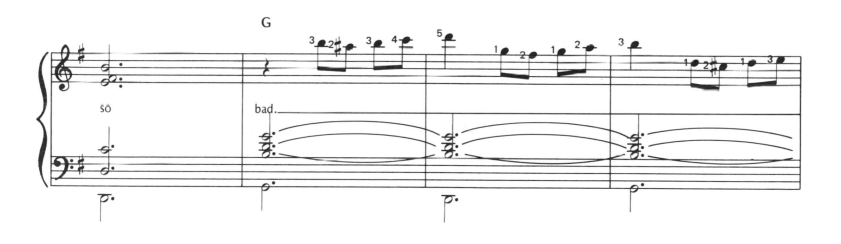

G

so   bad.

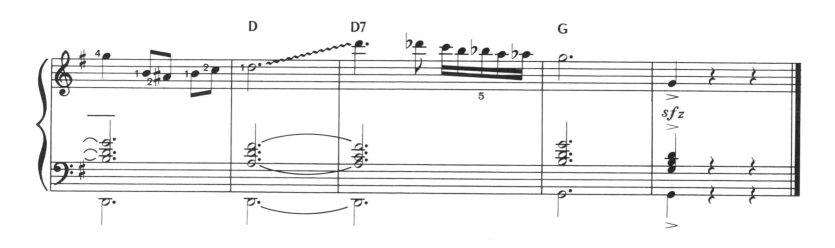

D   D7   G

sfz

Moonlight In Vermont

Electronic Organs
Upper: Flutes (or Tibias) 16', 4'
        Trombone
        Trumpet
Lower: Flute 8', Diapason 8'
        Reed 8'
Pedal: 8'
Vib./Trem.: On, Fast

Drawbar Organs
Upper: 82 5864 200
Lower: (00) 7103 000
Pedal: 06
Vib./Trem.: On, Fast

Words and Music by John Blackburn
and Karl Suessdorf

Lyrics:
Pen-nies in a stream, fall-ing leaves, a sy-ca-more, moon-light in Ver-mont. I-cy fin-ger- waves, ski trails on a moun-tain side, snow-light in Ver-mont, Tel-e-graph ca-bles they

My Funny Valentine

from BABES IN ARMS

Electronic Organs
Upper: Flutes (or Tibias) 16′, 8′, 4′, 2²/₃′
Lower: Flutes 8′, 4′
Pedal: 8′, Sustain
Vib./Trem.: Off

Drawbar Organs
Upper: 75 8860 000
Lower: (00) 6624 042
Pedal: 44 String Bass
Vib./Trem.: Off

Words by Lorenz Hart
Music by Richard Rodgers

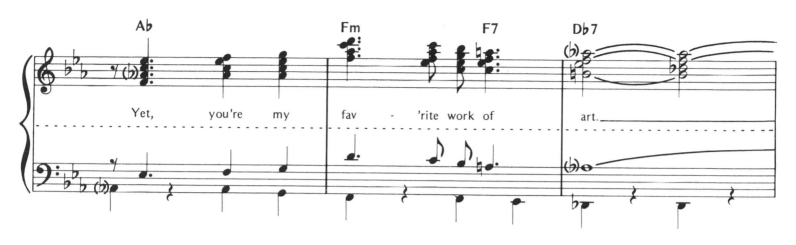

Yet, you're my fav - 'rite work of art.___

Is your fig - ure less than Greek; Is your

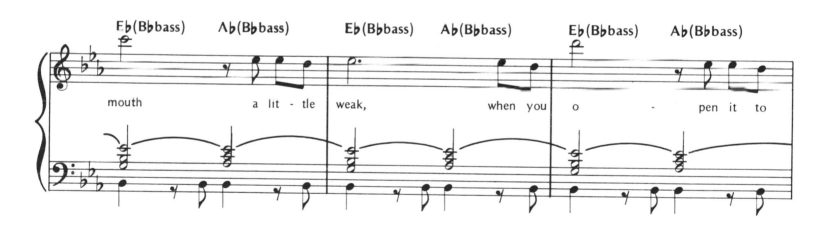

mouth a lit - tle weak, when you o - pen it to

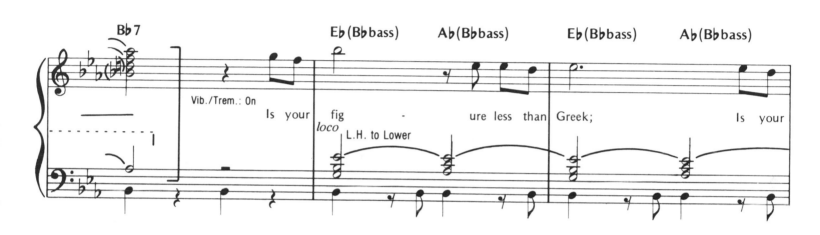

speak, Are you smart? But

On A Clear Day
(You Can See Forever)

Electronic Organs
Upper: Flutes (or Tibias) 16′, 8′,
    5⅓′, 4′, 2′
Lower: Flute 4′, Diapason 8′
Pedal: String Bass
Vib./Trem.: On, Slow

Drawbar Organs
Upper: 85 0000 345
Lower: (00) 5200 006
Pedal: String Bass
Vib./Trem.: On, Slow

Lyrics by Alan Jay Lerner
Music by Burton Lane

On The Street Where You Live

from MY FAIR LADY

Electronic Organs
Upper: Flutes (or Tibias) 16', 8', 4', 2'
      String 8', Clarinet
Lower: Flute 8', 4'
Pedal: 16', 8'
Vib./Trem.: On, Slow

Drawbar Organs
Upper: 80 8104 103
Lower: (00) 6303 004
Pedal: 25
Vib./Trem.: On, Slow

Words by Alan Jay Lerner
Music by Frederick Loewe

Moderately

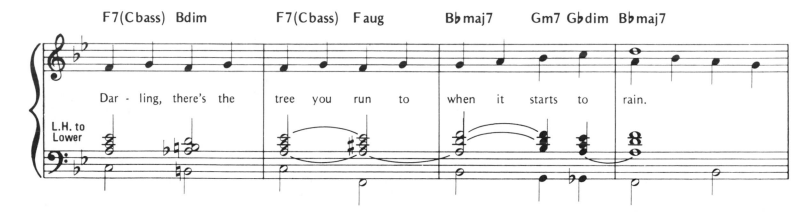

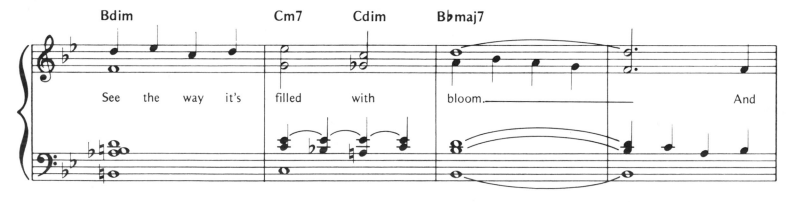

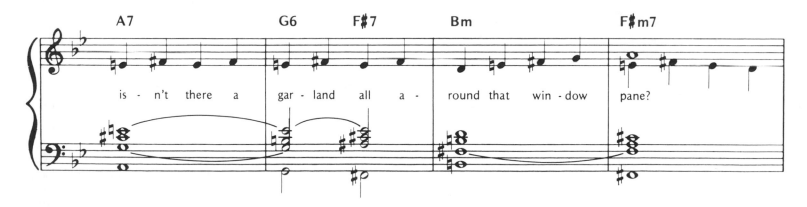

People
from FUNNY GIRL

Electronic Organs

Upper: Flutes (or Tibias) 8', 4'
Lower: Horn 8', String 8'
Pedal: 16', Sustain
Vib./Trem: On, Slow

Drawbar Organs

Upper: 00 7405 000
Lower: (00) 6787 542
Pedal: 50, Sustain
Vib./Trem.: On, Slow

Words by Bob Merrill
Music by Jule Styne

Satin Doll

Electronic Organs
Upper: Flutes (or Tibias) 16', 8', 5⅓', 4', 2'
Lower: Flute 4', Diapason 8'
Pedal: String Bass
Vib./Trem.: On, Slow

Drawbar Organs
Upper: 85 0000 355
Lower: (00) 8401 007
Pedal: String Bass
Vib./Trem.: On, Slow

Words by Johnny Mercer
Music by Billy Strayhorn and Duke Ellington

Some Enchanted Evening
from SOUTH PACIFIC

Electronic Organs
Upper: Flutes (or Tibias) 8′, 4′
       String 8′
Lower: Flute 8′
       String 8′
Pedal: 8′
Vib./Trem.: On, Fast

Drawbar Organs
Upper: 20 7702 000
Lower: (00) 7503 000
Pedal: 04
Vib./Trem.: On, Fast

Lyrics by Oscar Hammerstein II
Music by Richard Rodgers

Save The Best For Last

Electronic Organs
Upper: Flutes (or Tibias) 8',4',2'   String 4'
Lower: Reeds
Pedal: ContraBass or 16',8'
Vib./Trem.: On, Fast

Drawbar Organs
Upper: 00 8888 000
Lower: (00) 6655 231
Pedal: 54
Vib./Trem.: On, Fast

Words and Music by Phil Galdston,
Jon Lind and Wendy Waldman

Send In The Clowns
from the Musical A LITTLE NIGHT MUSIC

Electronic Organs
Upper: Flutes (or Tibias) 16', 4',
      String 8'
Lower: Flutes 8', 4', Diapason 8'
Pedal: String Bass
Vib./Trem.: On, Fast

Drawbar Organs
Upper: 60 3616 113
Lower: (00) 7634 212
Pedal: String Bass
Vib./Trem.: On, Fast

Music and Lyrics by
Stephen Sondheim

September Song

from the Musical Production KNICKERBOCKER HOLIDAY

Electronic Organs

Upper: String 8', Flute (or Tibia) 4'
Lower: String 8', Flute 8'
Pedal: 16', 8', Sustain
Vib./Trem: On

Drawbar Organs

Upper: 04 8800 402
Lower: (00) 5642 000
Pedal: 41, Sustain
Vib./Trem.: On

Words by Maxwell Anderson
Music by Kurt Weill

Somewhere Out There
from AN AMERICAN TAIL

Electronic Organs

Upper: Vibes or Orchestra Bells
      Sustain Upper Long
Lower: Strings 8', 4'
Pedal: 16', 8'
Vib./Trem.: On, Fast

Drawbar Organs

Upper: Vibes Prest or 80 0400 100
      Sustain, Add Percuss
Lower: (00) 5115, 113
Pedal: 43
Vib./Trem.: On, Fast

Words and Music by James Horner,
Barry Mann and Cynthia Weil

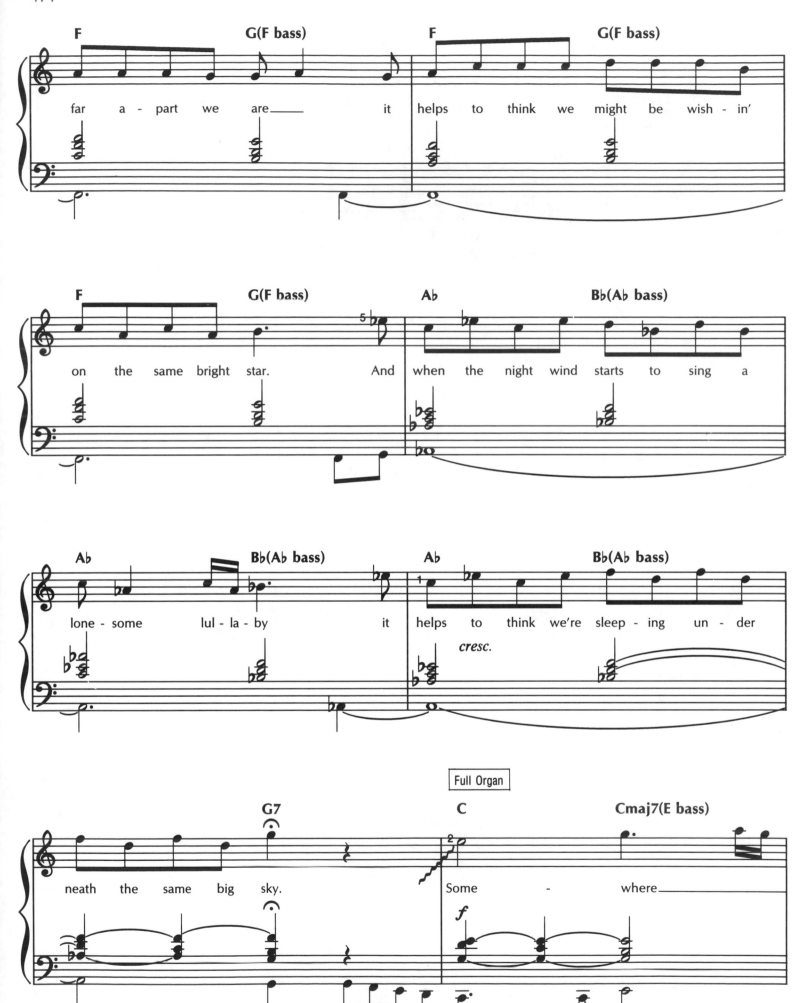

The Sound Of Music

from THE SOUND OF MUSIC

Electronic Organs

Upper: Flute (or Tibia) 8', Diapason 8',
      String 8'
Lower: Flutes 8', 4'
Pedal: 8'
Vib./Trem.: On, Fast

Drawbar Organs

Upper: 30 8320 000
Lower: (00) 6501 000
Pedal: 24
Vib./Trem.: On, Fast

Lyrics by Oscar Hammerstein II
Music by Richard Rodgers

Spanish Eyes

Electronic Organs
Upper: Kinura 16' (or Sax) Flute 4'
Lower: Flute 8' Reed 4'
Pedal: 16' Bass Gtr. 8'
Vib./Trem.: Full

Drawbar Organs
Upper: 83 0313 003
Lower: (00) 6303 002
Pedal: 04
Vib./Trem.: On, Fast

Words by Charles Singleton
and Eddie Snyder
Music by Bert Kaempfert

St. Louis Blues

Electronic Organs
Upper: Jazz Organ with Percussion
Lower: Jazz Sounds
Pedal: String Bass 8'
Vib./Trem.: Slow

Drawbar Organs
Upper: 83 6030 400
Add Percussion
Lower: (00) 6402 003
Pedal: String Bass
Vib./Trem.: Slow

Words and Music by
W.C. Handy

I hate to see ___ de ev'-nin' sun go
Been to de Gyp-sy to get ma for - tune
You ought to see ___ dat stove-pipe brown of

down, _____ hate to see ___
tole, _____ to de Gyp-sy
mine _____ lak he owns _

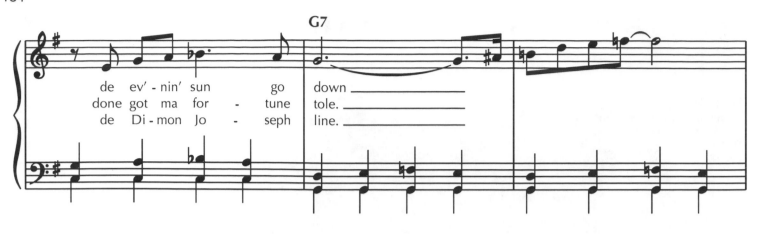

de ev'-nin' sun go down _____
done got ma for - tune tole. _____
de Di-mon Jo - seph line. _____

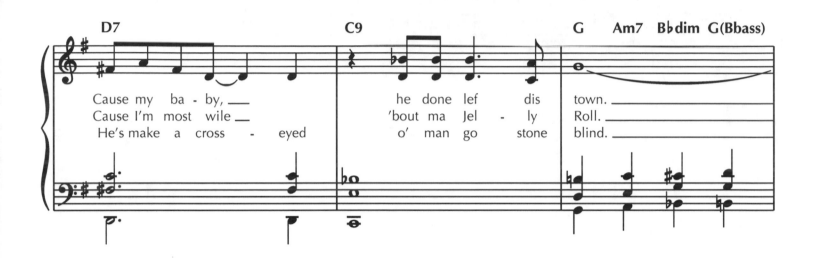

Cause my ba - by, ___ he done lef dis town. _____
Cause I'm most wile ___ 'bout ma Jel - ly Roll. _____
He's make a cross - eyed o' man go stone blind. _____

___ Feel-in' to-mor - row lak ___ Ah feel to -
___ Gyp - sy done tole ___ me "Don't ___ you wear no
___ Black-er than mid - night, teeth ___ like flags of

day _____ feel to-mor - row
black." _____ Yes, she done tole me
truce _____ black - est ___ man

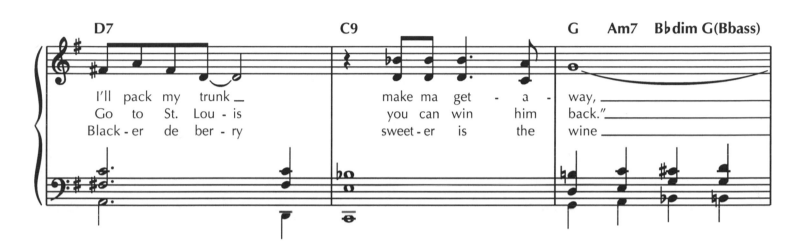

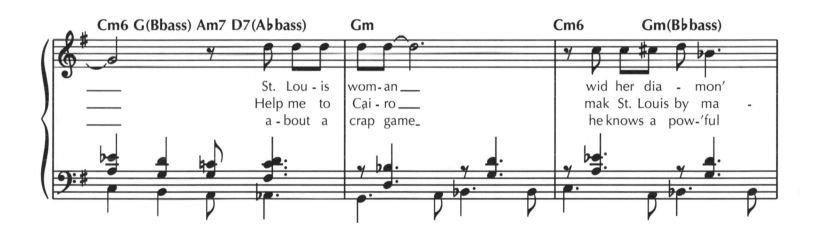

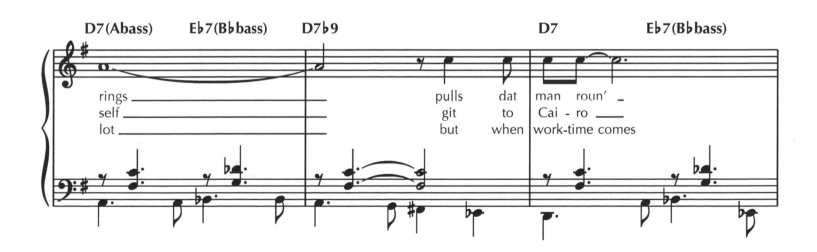

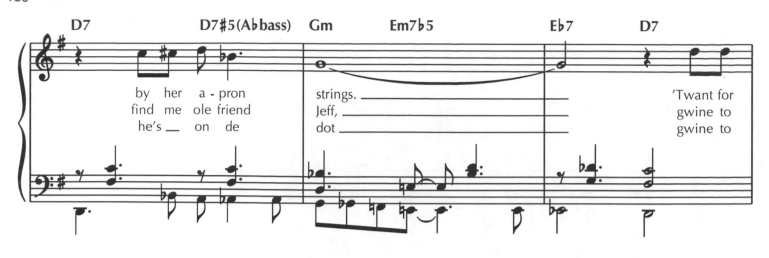

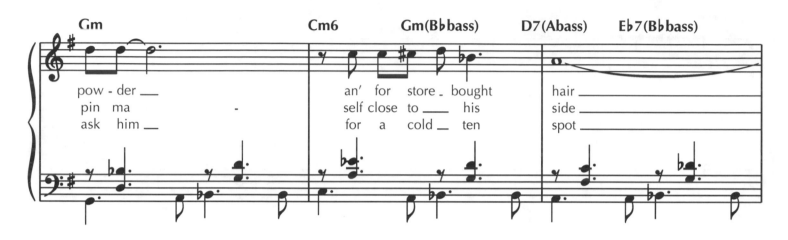

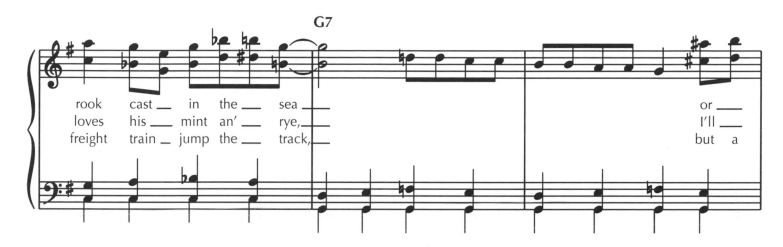

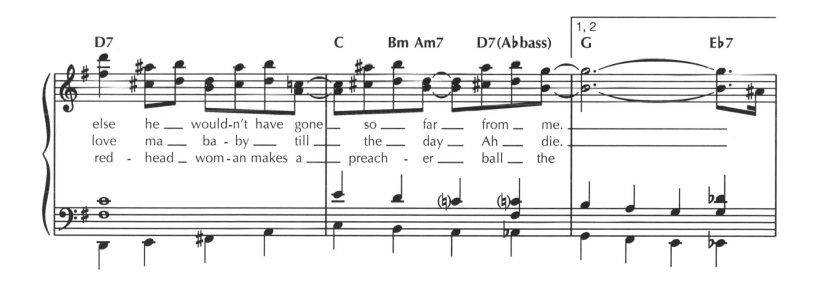

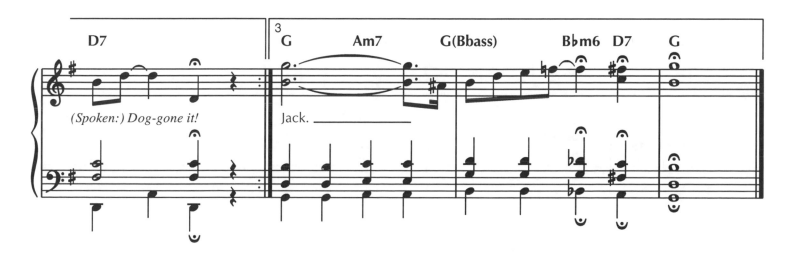

Speak Softly, Love

Love Theme from the Paramount Motion Picture THE GODFATHER

Electronic Organs
Upper: Oboe, Flute
Lower: Strings
Pedal: 16', 8' (sust.)
Vib./Trem.: Slow

Drawbar Organs
Upper: 80 7003 051
Lower: (00) 7303 004
Pedal: String Bass
Vib./Trem.: On, Slow

Words by Larry Kusik
Music by Nino Rota

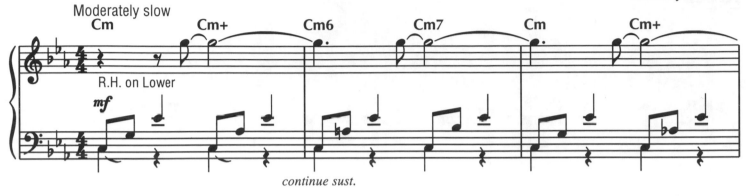

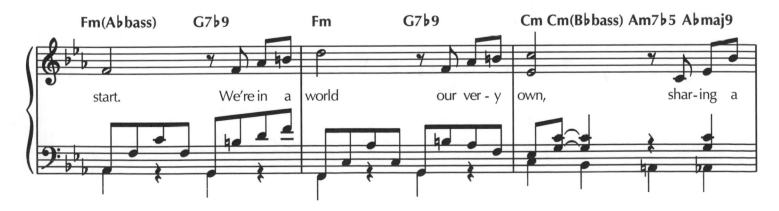

Stormy Weather
(Keeps Rainin' All The Time)

Electronic Organs
Upper: Saxophone
Lower: Flute 8', Reed 8'
Pedal: Flute 8', Guitar 8'(sust.)
Vib./Trem.: Slow

Drawbar Organs
Upper: 81 5355 130
Lower: (00) 8303 001
Pedal: 04
Vib./Trem.: On, Slow

Lyric by Ted Koehler
Music by Harold Arlen

Strangers In The Night
Adapted from A MAN COULD GET KILLED

Electronic Organs

Upper: Flutes (or Tibias) 16', 8', 4', 2'
Lower: Flutes 8', 4', Diapason 8'
Pedal: String Bass
Vib./Trem.: On, Slow

Drawbar Organs

Upper: 80 6606 000
Lower: (00) 7400 000
Pedal: String Bass
Vib./Trem.: On, Slow

Words by Charles Singleton and Eddie Snyder
Music by Bert Kaempfert

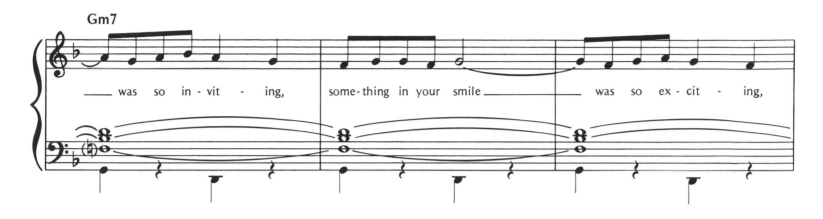

Lit - tle did we know love was just a glance a - way, a warm em - brac - ing dance a - way and

ev - er since that night we've been to - geth - er, lov - ers at first sight

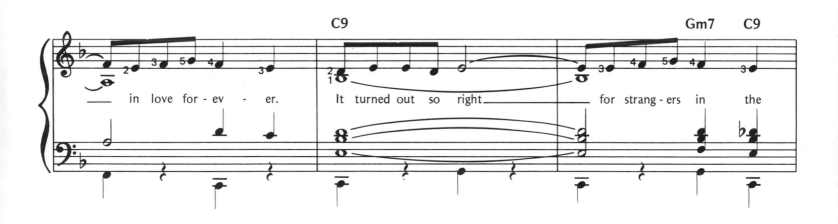

in love for - ev - er. It turned out so right for strang - ers in the

night. night.

A String Of Pearls

Electronic Organs

Upper: Flutes (or Tibias) 16', 8', 5⅓', 4', 2'
Lower: Flutes 8', 4', Diapason 8', Reed 8'
Pedal: 16', 8'
Vib./Trem.: On, Fast

Drawbar Organs

Upper: 86 6606 000
Lower: (00) 7732 211
Pedal: 55
Vib./Trem.: On, Fast

Words by Eddie DeLange
Music by Jerry Gray

With a bright swing feel

Lyrics under the staves:

Ba - by Here's a five and dime, Ba - by Now's a - bout the time

For a string of pearls a - la Wool - worth.

Ev - 'ry pearl's a star a - bove wrapped in dreams and filled with love

Summertime
from PORGY AND BESS

Electronic Organs

Upper: Flutes (or Tibias) 16', 8', 5 1/3', 4', 2'
Lower: Flute 4', Diapason 8'
Pedal: String Bass
Vib./Trem: On, Slow

Drawbar Organs

Upper: 85 0000 355
Lower: (00) 8401 007
Pedal: String Bass
Vib./Trem.: On, Slow

Words and Music by George Gershwin,
Du Bose and Dorothy Heyward and Ira Gershwin

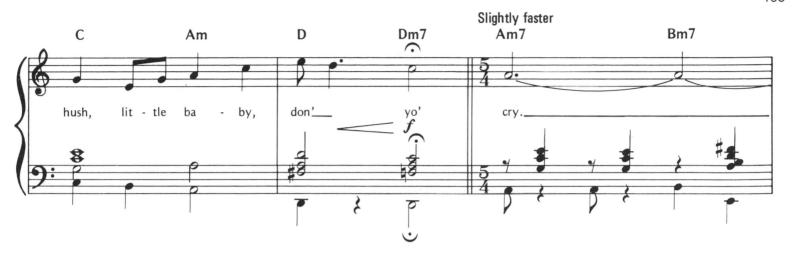

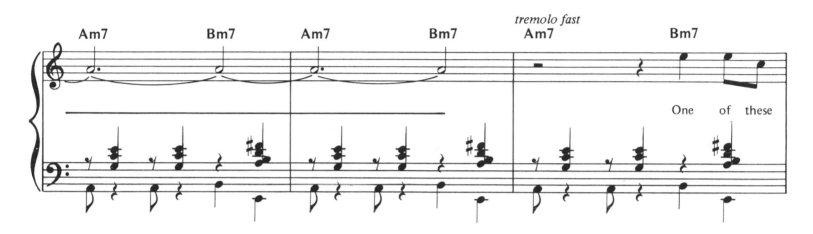

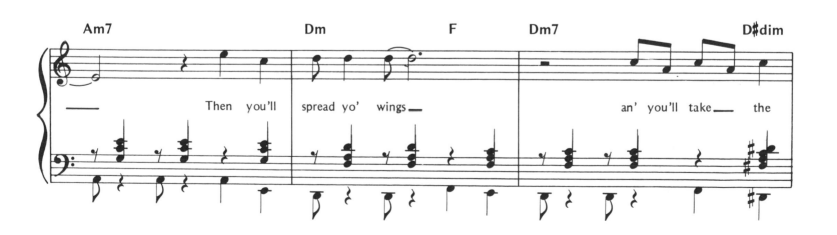

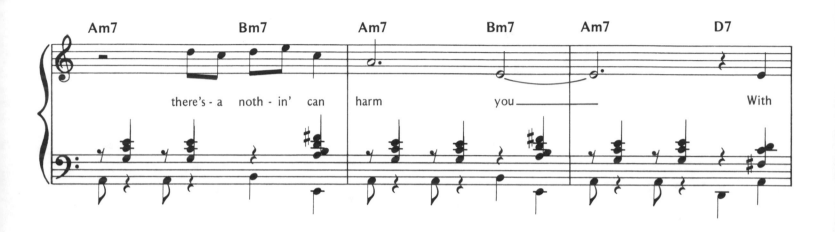

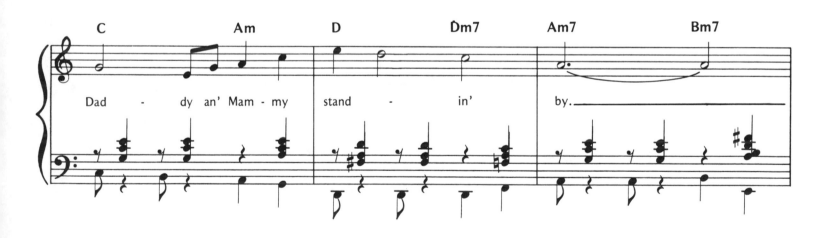

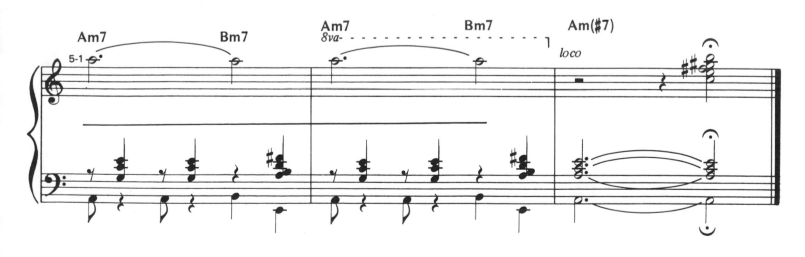

Sunrise, Sunset
from the Musical FIDDLER ON THE ROOF

Electronic Organs
Upper: Flute (or Tibia) 4', Oboe 8'
Lower: Flute 8', String 8'
Pedal: 8'
Vib./Trem.: On, Fast

Drawbar Organs
Upper: 00 6640 000
Lower: (00) 5323 001
Pedal: 34
Vib./Trem.: On, Fast

Lyrics by Sheldon Harnick
Music by Jerry Bock

get to be a beau - ty? When did he grow to be so
ring a - round her fin - ger. Share the sweet wine and break so the

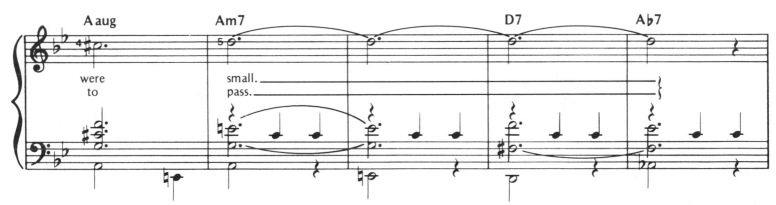

tall? Was - n't it yes - ter - day when they
glass; Soon the full cir - cle will when have come

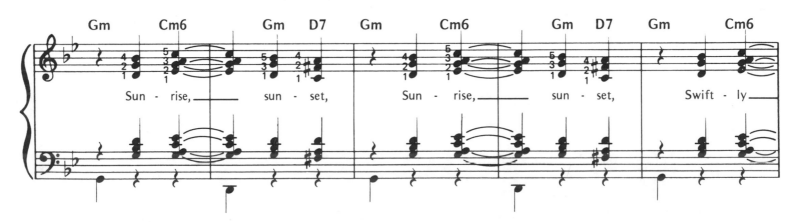

were to small. _____
to pass. _____

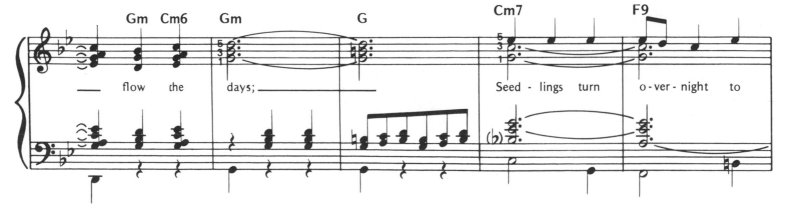

Sun - rise, _____ sun - set, Sun - rise, _____ sun - set, Swift - ly
_____ flow the days; _____ Seed - lings turn o - ver - night to

Tears In Heaven

Electronic Organs
Upper: Flutes (or Tibias) 8', 4'
Lower: String 8'
Pedal: 16', 8'
Vib./Trem.: On, Fast

Drawbar Organs
Upper: 00 8008 000
Lower: (00) 6322 441
Pedal: 52
Vib./Trem.: On, Fast

Words and Music by Eric Clapton
and Will Jennings

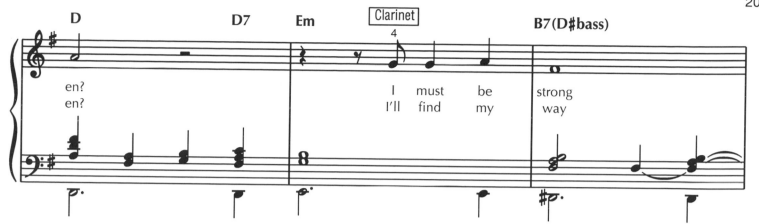

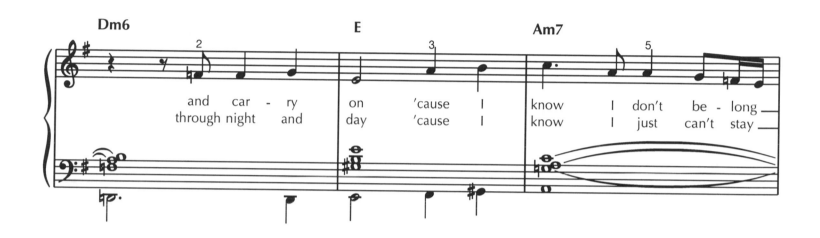

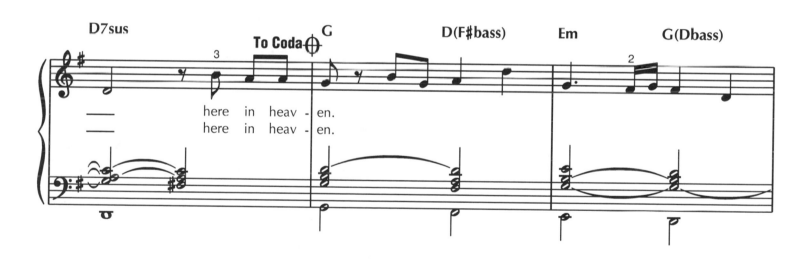

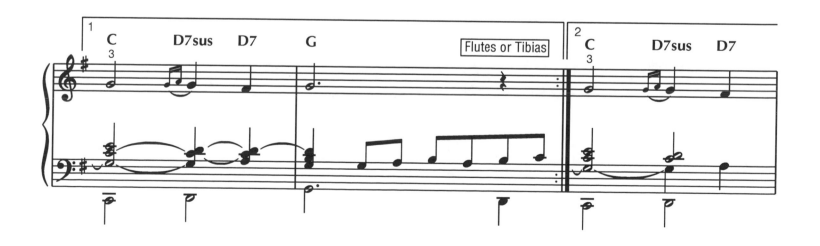

Three Coins In The Fountain

Electronic Organs
Upper: Flutes (or Tibias) 16', 8', 2'
       Diapason 8', String 8'
Lower: Flutes 8', 4', String 8'
Pedal: Bourdon 16', String Bass
Vib./Trem.: On, Slow

Drawbar Organs
Upper: 80 8868 550
Lower: (00) 7704 000
Pedal: 64
Vib./Trem.: On, Slow

Words by Sammy Cahn
Music by Jule Styne

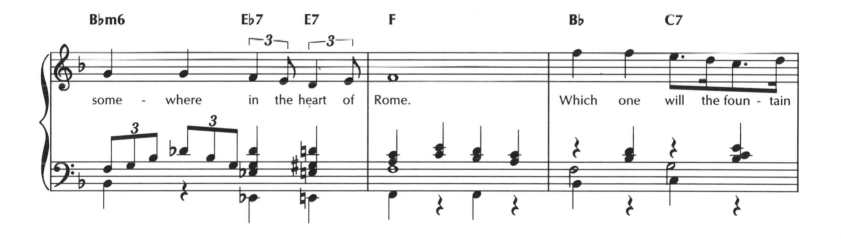

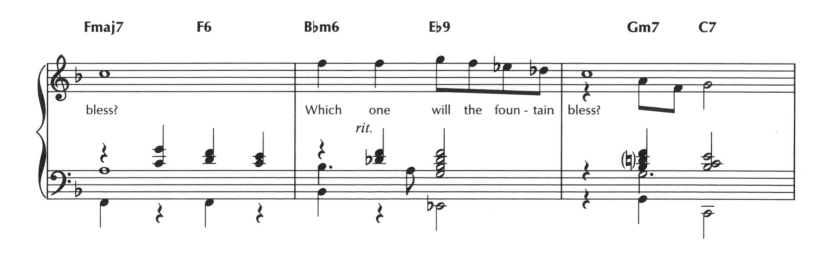

Through The Years

Electronic Organs
Upper: Flutes (or Tibias) 16', 8', 4',
       Trumpet, Oboe
Lower: Flutes 8', 4', String 8',
       Reed 8'
Pedal: 16', 8'
Vib./Trem.: On, Fast

Drawbar Organs
Upper: 80 7766 008
Lower: (00) 8076 000
Pedal: 36
Vib./Trem: On, Fast

Words and Music by Steve Dorff
and Marty Panzer

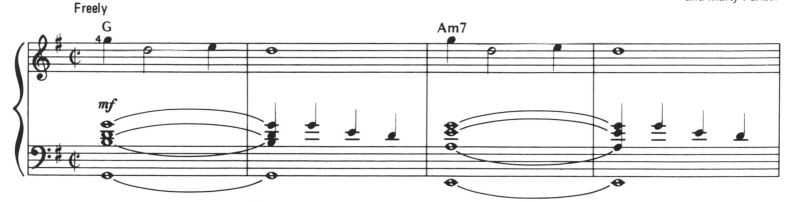

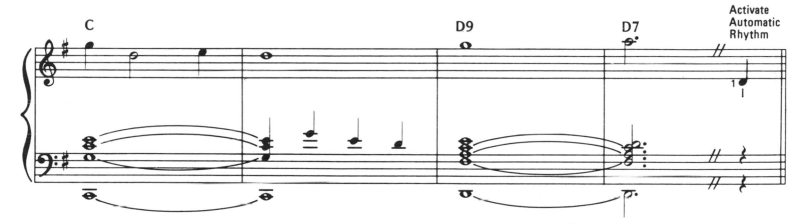

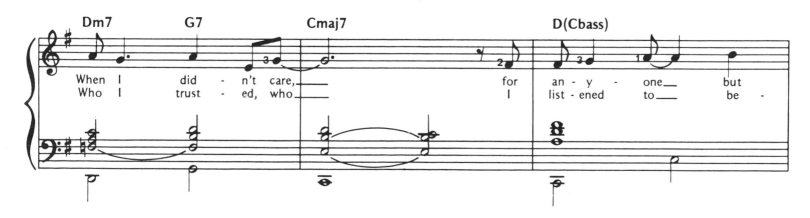

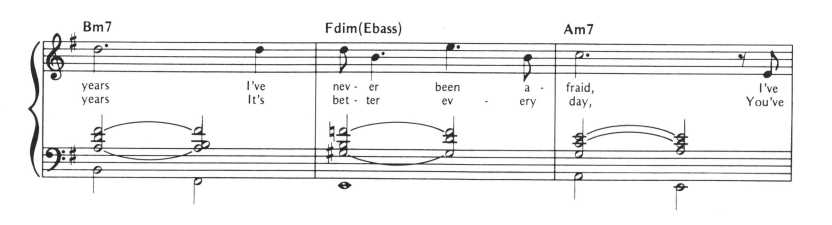

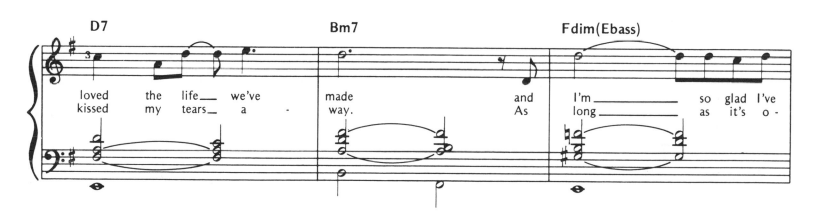

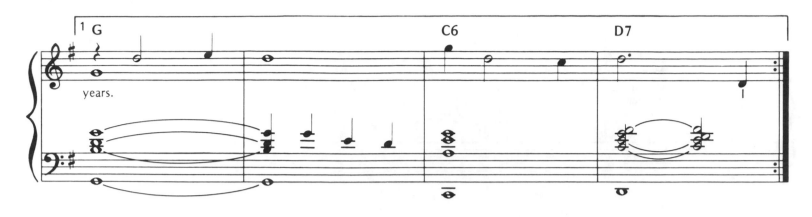

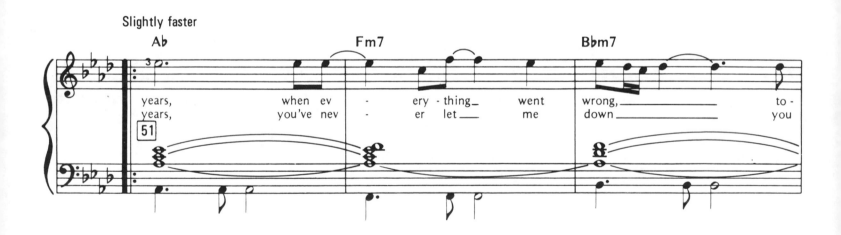

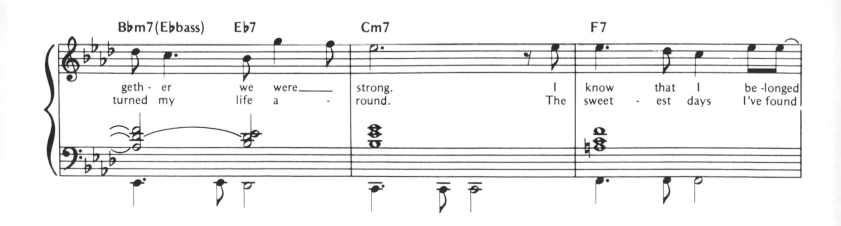

215

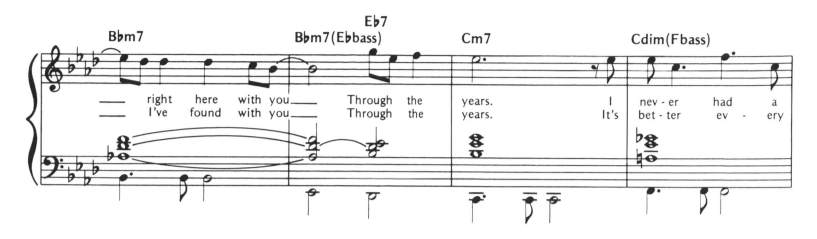

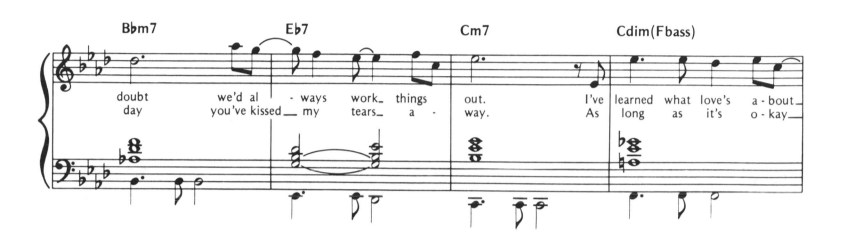

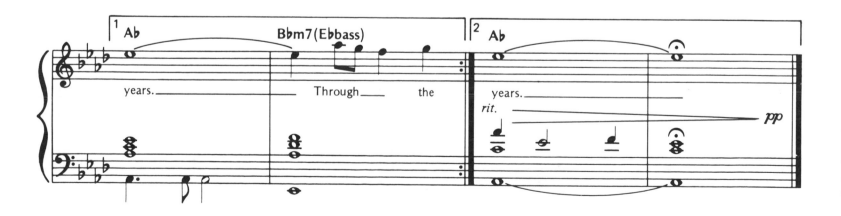

A Time For Us
Love Theme from the Paramount Picture ROMEO AND JULIET

Electronic Organs
Upper: Clarinet 8'
Lower: Flute 8'
Pedal: Flute 8'
Vib./Trem.: Slow

Drawbar Organs
Upper: 80 8104 103
Lower: (00) 6303 004
Pedal: 25
Vib./Trem.: On, Slow

Words by Larry Kusik and Eddie Snyder
Music by Nino Rota

True Love
from HIGH SOCIETY

Electronic Organs
Upper: Flutes (or Tibias) 16′, 4′, String 8′
Lower: Flutes 8′, 4′, Diapason 8′
Pedal: String Bass
Vib./Trem.: On, Fast

Drawbar Organs
Upper: 60 3616 113
Lower: (00) 7634 212
Pedal: String Bass
Vib./Trem.: On, Fast

Words and Music by
Cole Porter

Moderately

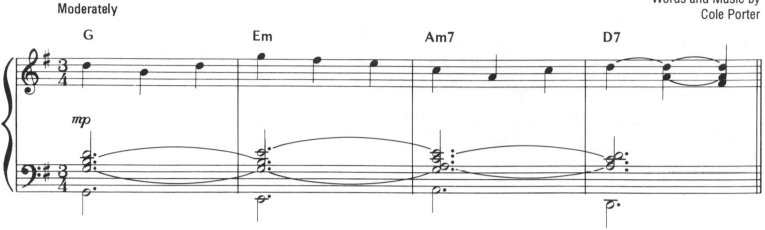

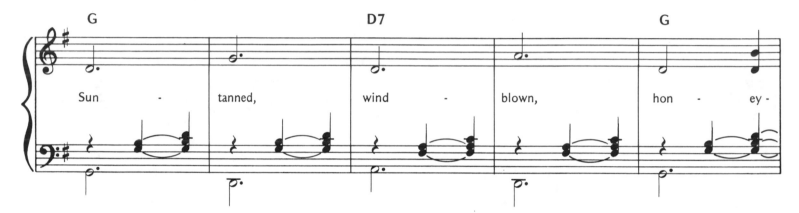

Sun - tanned, wind - blown, hon - ey -

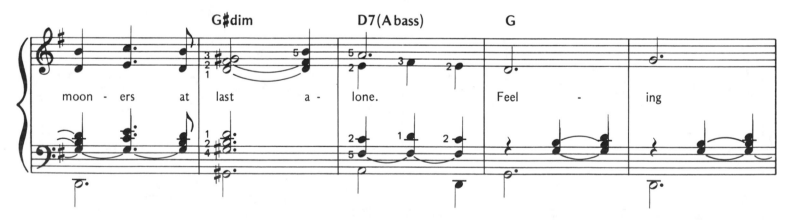

moon - ers at last a - lone. Feel - ing

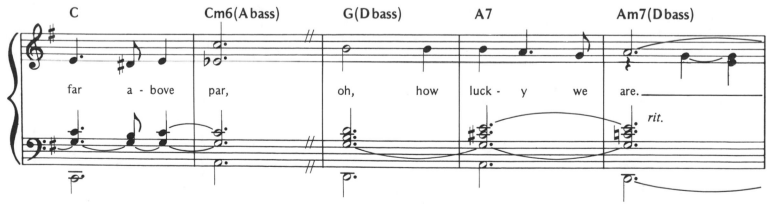

far a - bove par, oh, how luck - y we are.

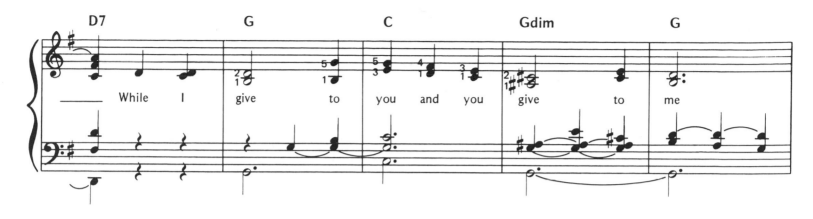

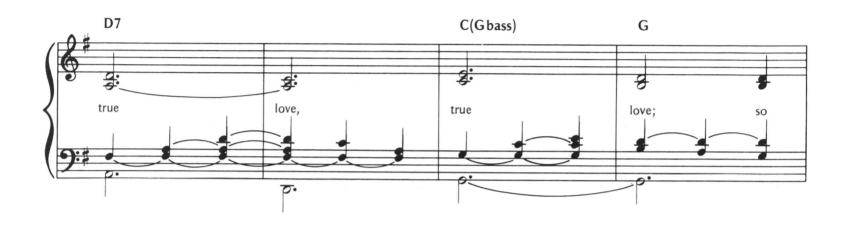

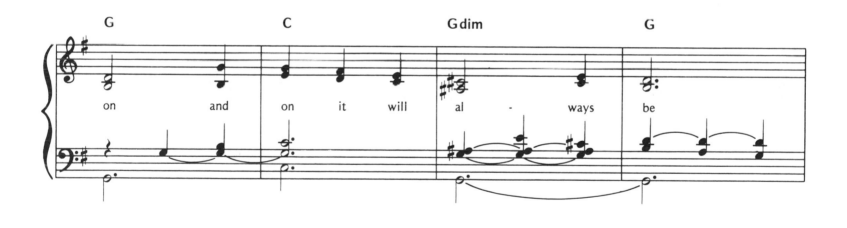

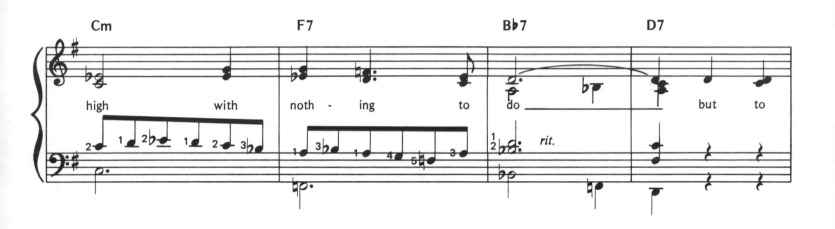

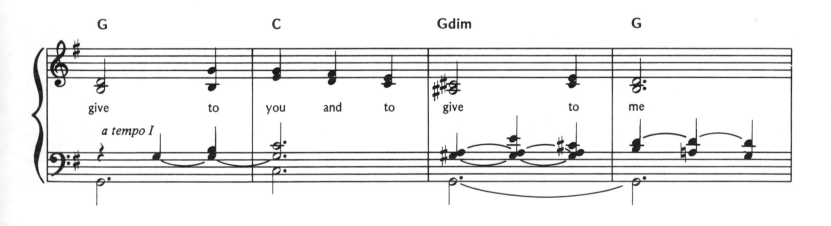

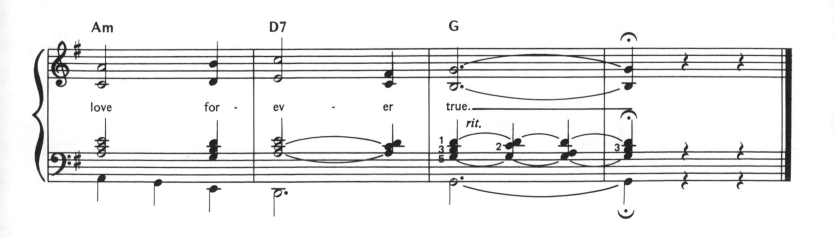

Try To Remember
from THE FANTASTICKS

Electronic Organs
Upper: Flutes (or Tibias) 16', 4', String 8'
Lower: Flutes 8', 4', Diapason 8'
Pedal: String Bass
Vib./Trem.: On, Fast

Drawbar Organs
Upper: 60 3616 113
Lower: (00) 7634 212
Pedal: String Bass
Vib./Trem.: On, Fast

Words by Tom Jones
Music by Harvey Schmidt

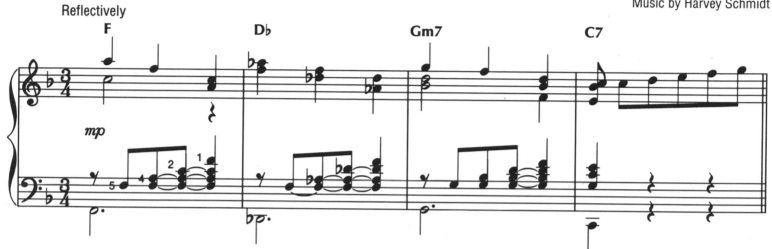

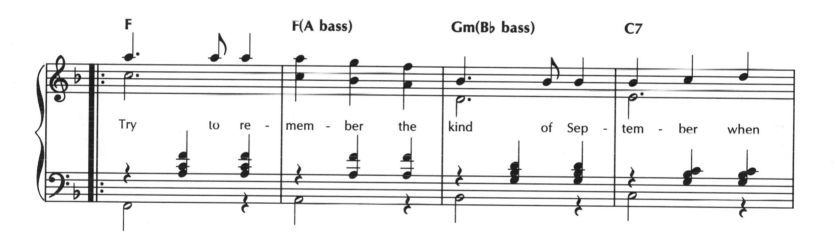

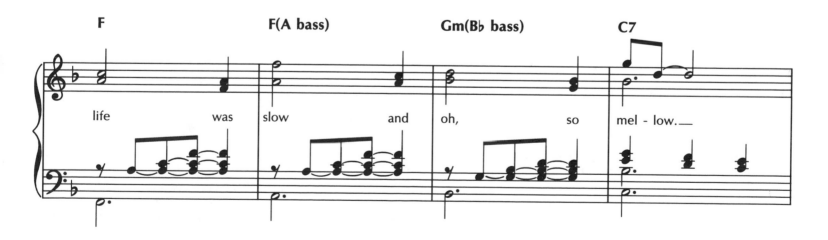

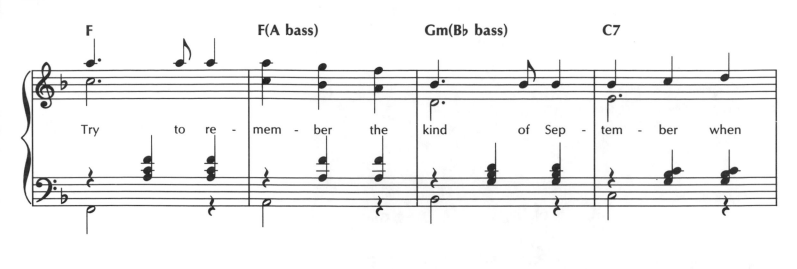

Try to re-mem-ber the kind of Sep-tem-ber when

grass was green and grain was yel-low.

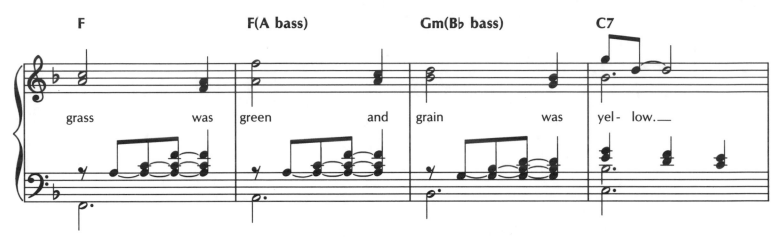

Try to re-mem-ber the kind of Sep-tem-ber when

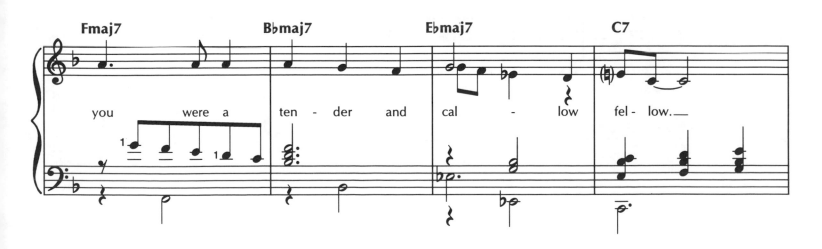

you were a ten-der and cal-low fel-low.

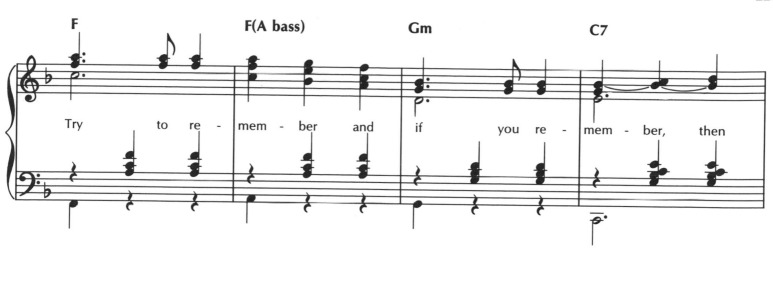

Try to re-mem-ber and if you re-mem-ber, then

fol-low.___ (Echo) Fol-low, fol-low, fol-low, fol-low, fol-low, fol-low, fol-low, fol-low,

dim. *rall.*

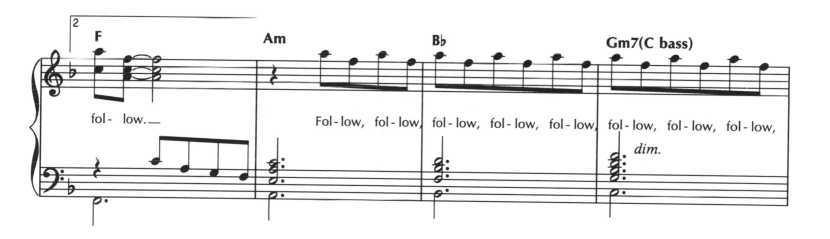

fol-low.___ Fol-low, fol-low, fol-low, fol-low, fol-low, fol-low, fol-low, fol-low,

dim.

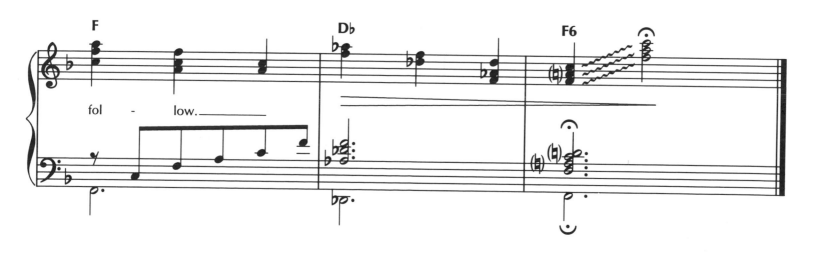

fol - low.___

Unchained Melody

Lyric by Hy Zaret
Music by Alex North

Registration 3

Slowly — Ad-Lib (with expression)

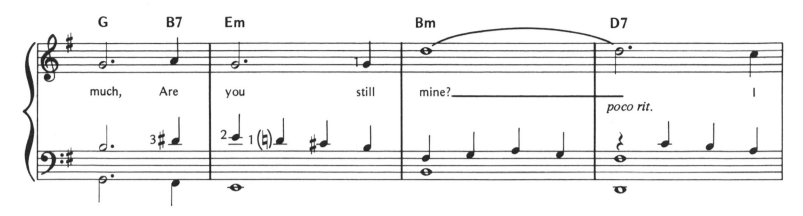

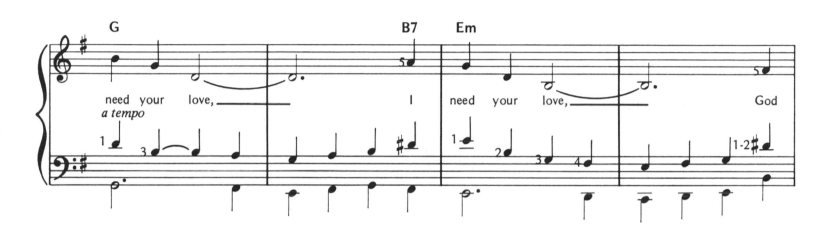

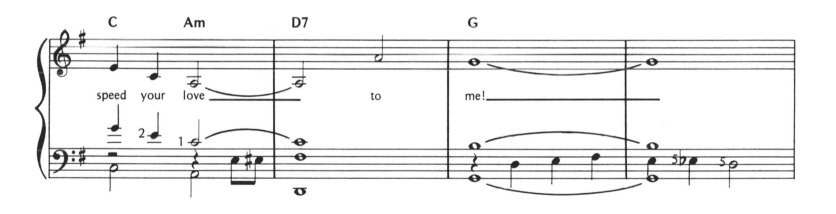

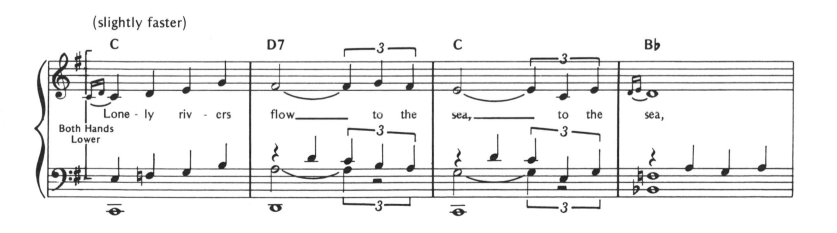

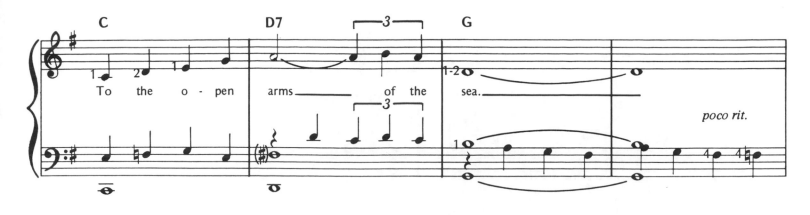

To the o - pen arms _____ of the sea. _____

poco rit.

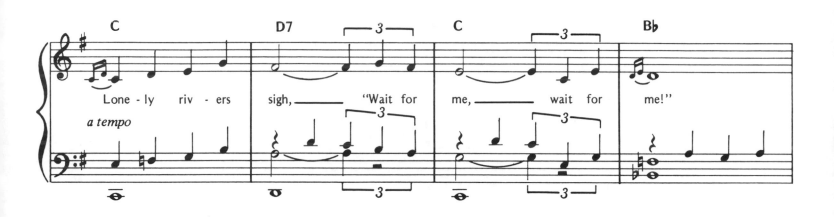

a tempo

Lone - ly riv - ers sigh, _____ "Wait for me, _____ wait for me!"

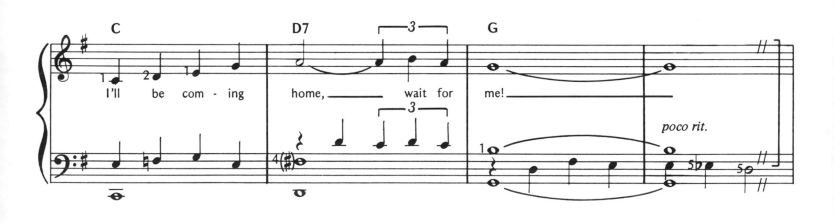

I'll be com - ing home, _____ wait for me!

poco rit.

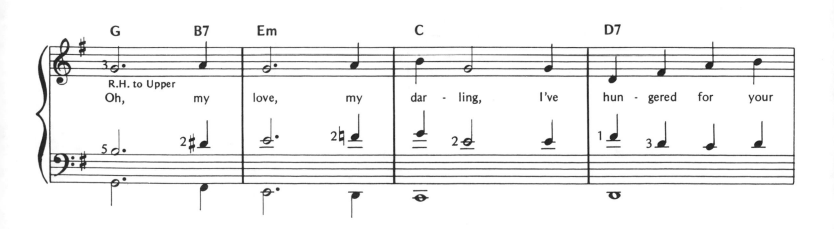

R.H. to Upper

Oh, my love, my dar - ling, I've hun - gered for your

The Way We Were
from the Motion Picture THE WAY WE WERE

Electronic Organs
Upper: Piano, Strings
Lower: Strings 8', Flute 4'
Pedal: Bass Guitar
Vib./Trem.: Medium Vib.

Drawbar Organs
Upper: 40 0006 000
Lower: (00) 4004 000
Pedal: 4 2
Vib./Trem.: On, Fast

Words by Alan and Marilyn Bergman
Music by Marvin Hamlisch

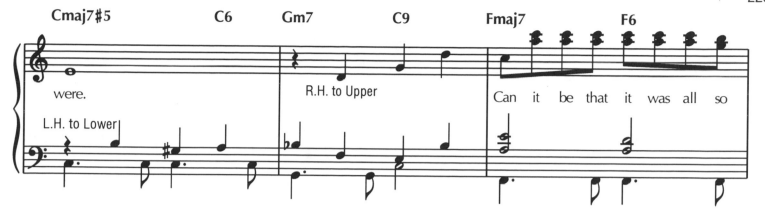

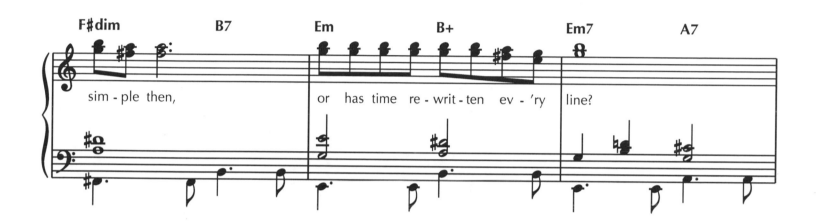

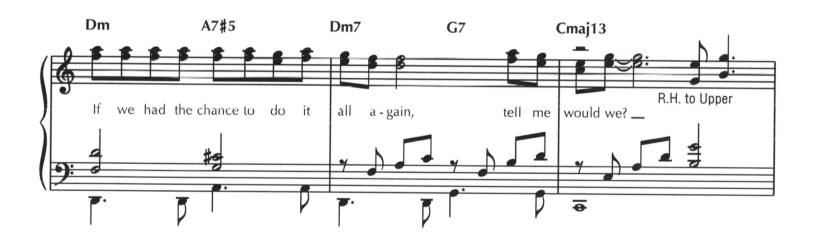

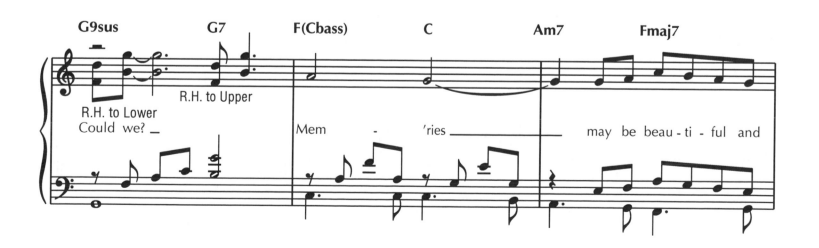

What A Wonderful World

Electronic Organs

Upper: Flutes (or Tibias) 16', 8', 4'
Lower: Melodia 8', Reed 8'
Pedal: 16', 8'
Vib./Trem.: On, Fast

Drawbar Organs

Upper: 80 4800 000
Lower: (00) 7334 011
Pedal: 25
Vib./Trem.: On, Fast

Words and Music by George David Weiss
and Bob Thiele

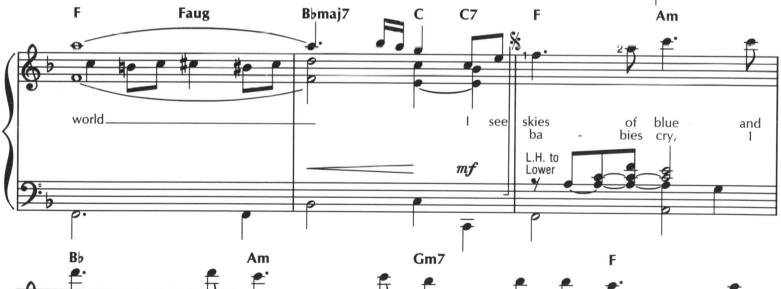

What Kind Of Fool Am I?

from the Musical Production STOP THE WORLD - I WANT TO GET OFF

Electronic Organs

Upper: Flutes (or Tibias) 8′, 4′, 2′
Lower: Flute 8′
        String 8′
Pedal: String Bass
Vib./Trem.: On, Fast

Drawbar Organs

Upper: 40 7706 000
Lower: (00) 7203 001
Pedal: 06
Vib./Trem.: On, Fast

Words and Music by Leslie Bricusse
and Anthony Newley

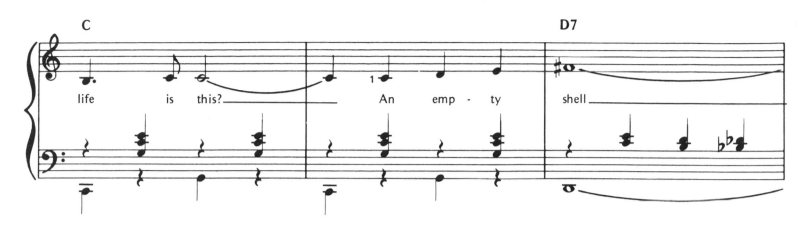

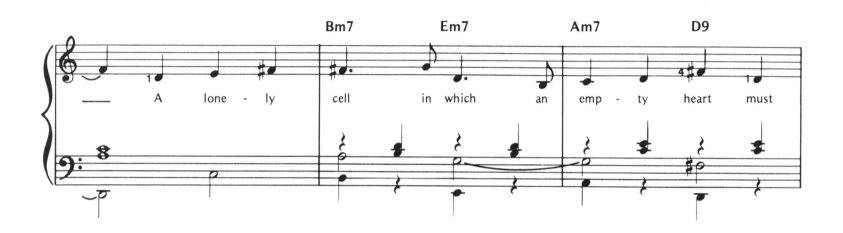

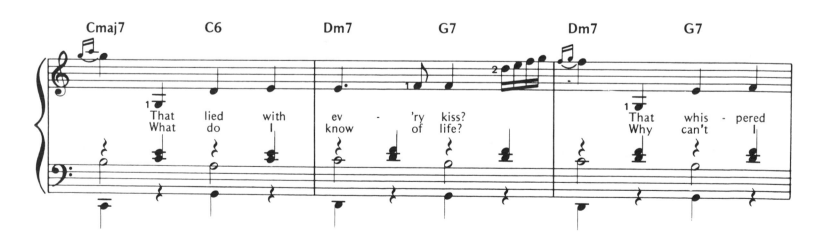

When I Fall In Love

Electronic Organs
Upper: Full Organ
Lower: Full Organ (8' only)
Pedal: Full
Vib./Trem.: Full

Drawbar Organs
Upper: 80 0800 000
Lower: (00) 5303 000
Pedal: 24
Vib./Trem.: On, Slow

Words by Edward Heyman
Music by Victor Young

Where Do I Begin
(Love Theme)
from the Paramount Picture LOVE STORY

Electronic Organs
Upper: Piano or Vibes
Lower: Flute 8', Strings 4'
Pedal: 16' 8'
Vib./Trem.: Off

Drawbar Organs
Upper: 80 6606 000
Lower: (00) 7400 000
Pedal: 24
Vib./Trem.: Off

Words by Carl Sigman
Music by Francis Lai

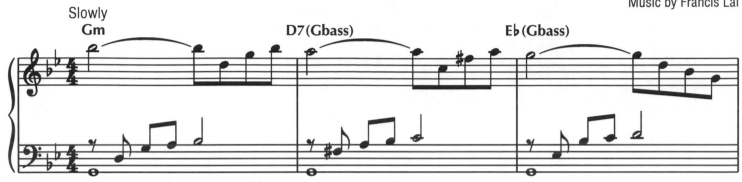

Where do I be-gin ___ to tell the sto-ry of how
With her first hel-lo ___ she gave a mean-ing to this

great a love can be, ___ the sweet love sto-ry that is old-er than the sea,
emp-ty world of mine. ___ There'd nev-er be an-oth-er love, an-oth-er time;

the sim-ple truth a-bout the love she brings to me?
she came in-to my life and made the liv-ing fine.

Where do I

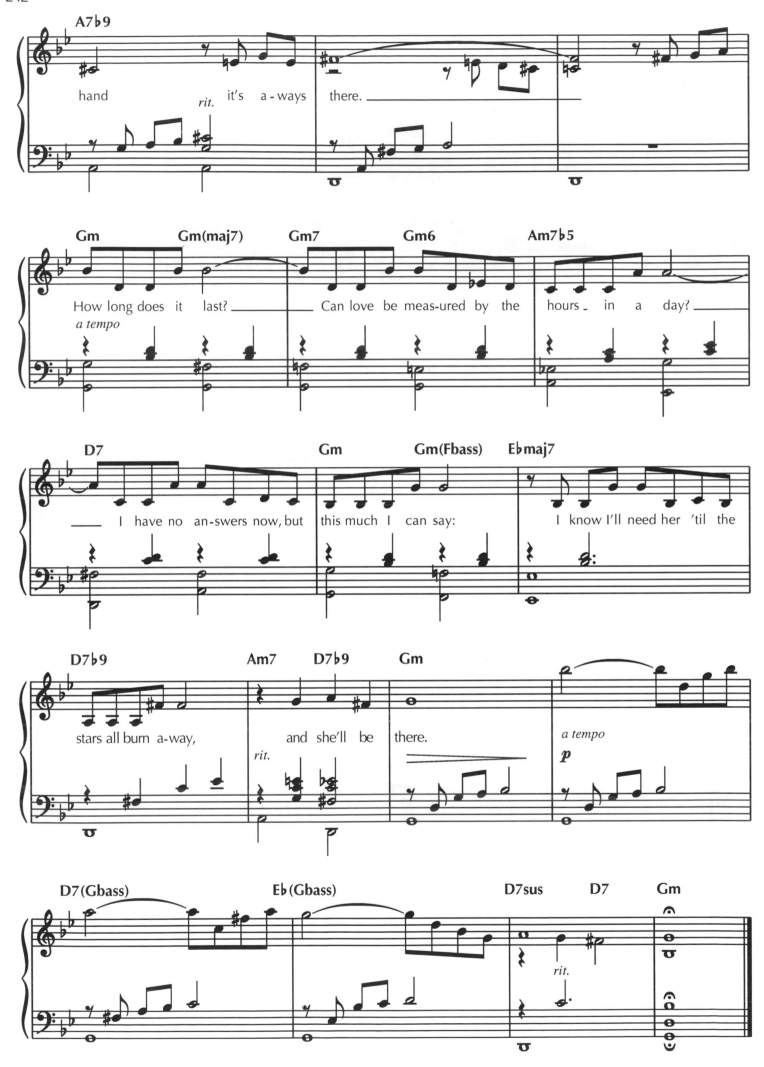

Yesterday

Electronic Organs
Upper: Flutes (or Tibias) 16′, 8′, 5⅓′,
     4′, 2′
Lower: Flutes 8′, 4′, Diapason 8′,
     Reed 8′
Pedal: 16′, 8′
Vib./Trem.: On, Fast

Tonebar Organs
Upper: 86 6606 000
Lower: (00) 7732 211
Pedal: 55
Vib./Trem.: On, Fast

Words and Music by John Lennon
and Paul McCartney

Slowly

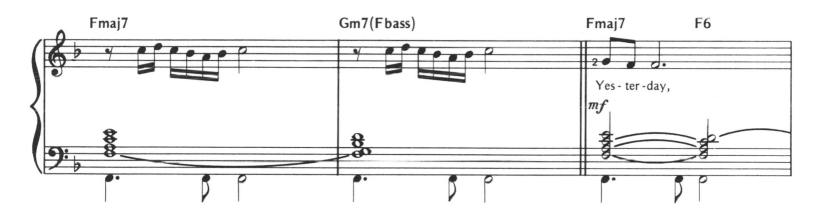

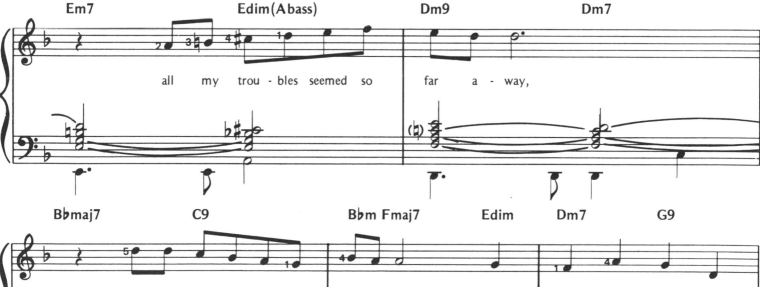

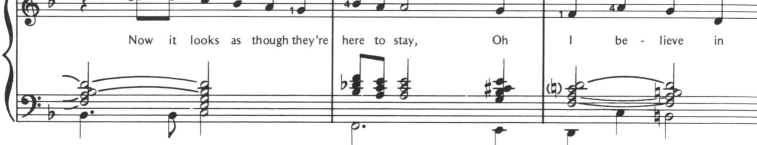

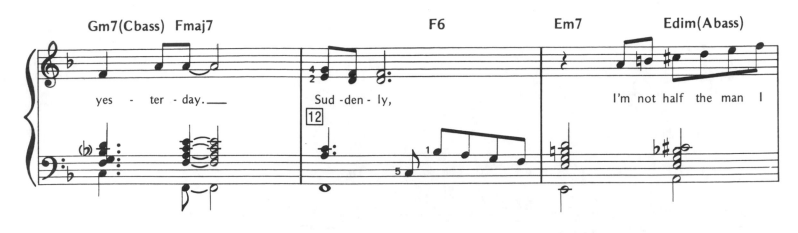

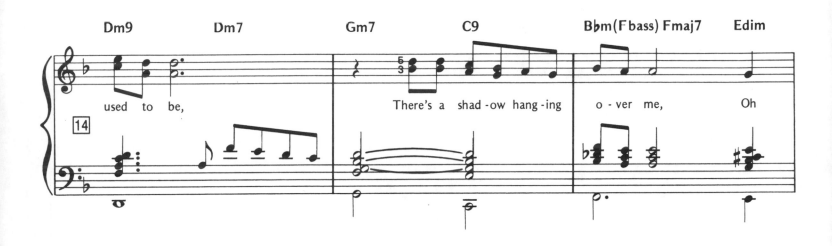

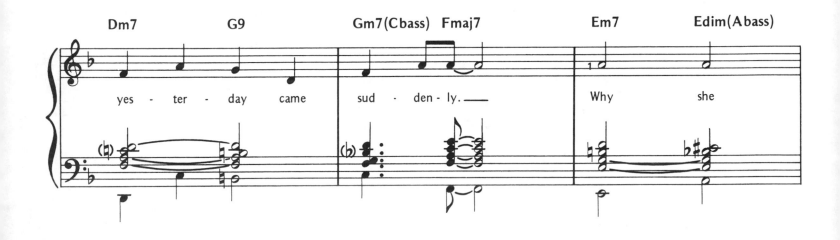

245

You Needed Me

Electronic Organs

Upper: Flutes (or Tibias) 16', 8', 4'
   Reed 8', Oboe 8'
Lower: Strings 8', 4'
   Flute 8' (opt.)
Pedal 16', 8'
Vib./Trem.: On, Fast

Drawbar Organs

Upper: 40 8402 000
Lower: (00) 4403 000
Pedal: 34
Vib./Trem.: On, Fast

Words and Music by
Randy Goodrum

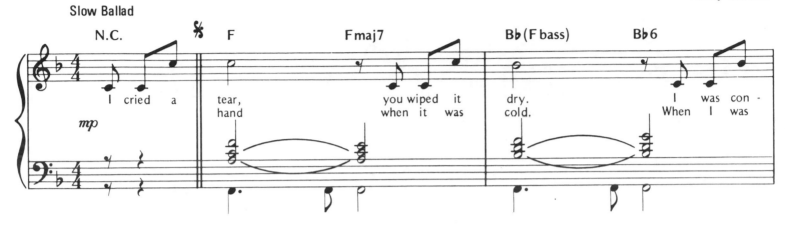

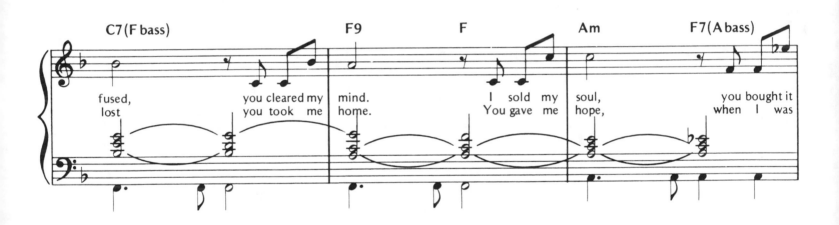

247

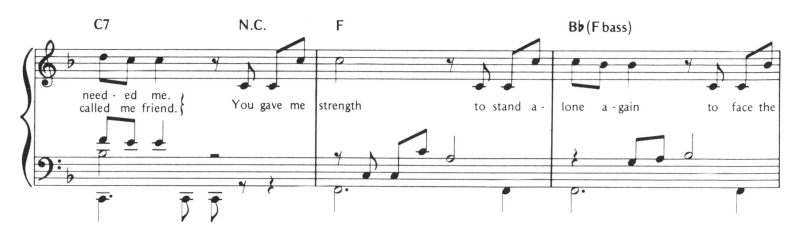

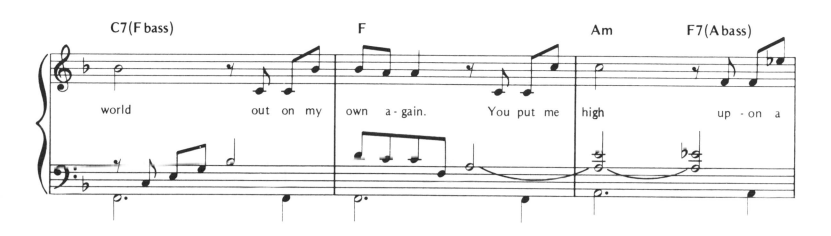

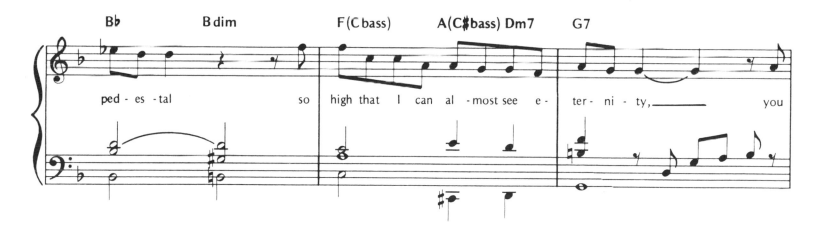

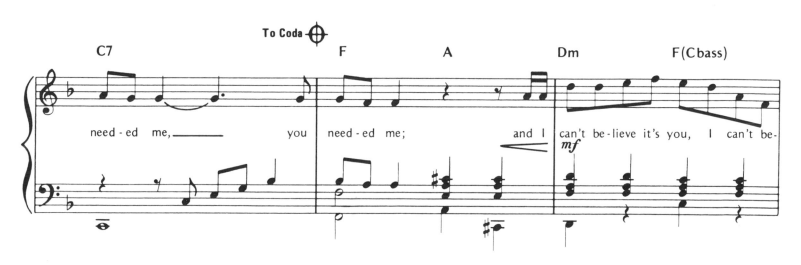

Your Song

Electronic Organs
Upper: Flutes (or Tibias) 16′, 8′, 4′, 2′,
       Strings 8′, 4′
Lower: Flutes 8′, 4′, Strings 8′, 4′
Pedal: 8′, Sustain
Vib./Trem.: On, Fast

Drawbar Organs
Upper: 80 7105 123
Lower: (00) 7314 003
Pedal: 25, Sustain
Vib./Trem.: On, Fast

Words and Music by Elton John
and Bernie Taupin

we both could live   this one's for you ___

CHORUS

And you can tell ev-'ry-bod - y   This___ is your song._____   It may___ be quite___ sim-ple but___

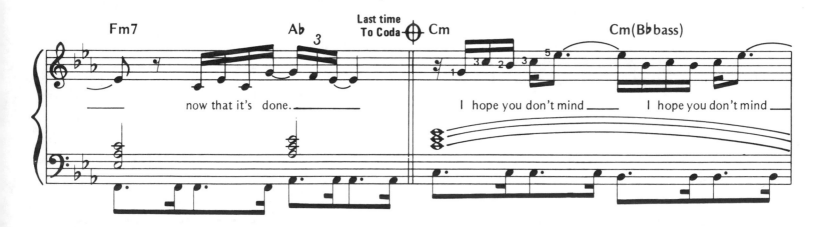

___ now that it's done._____   I hope you don't mind _____ I hope you don't mind ___

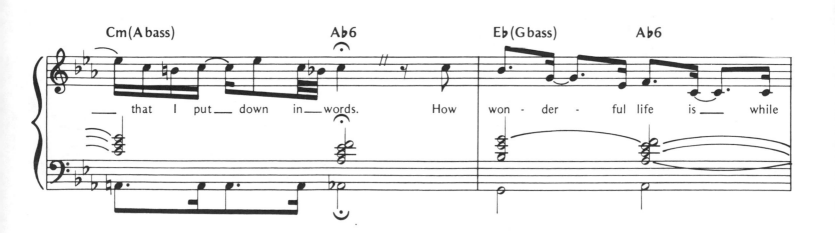

___ that I put___ down in___ words.   How won - der - ful life is ___ while

you're— in the world—

I hope you don't mind,— I hope you don't mind—

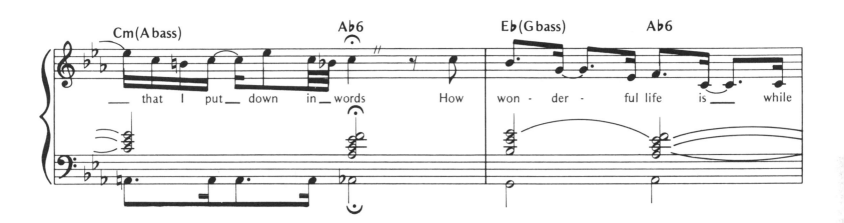

—— that I put— down in —words   How   won - der - ful life   is ___   while

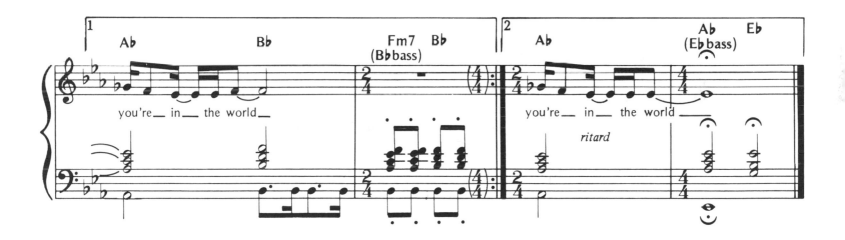

you're— in— the world—

you're— in— the world ——

ritard

3. I sat on the roof
    and kicked off the moss,
    well a few of the verses,
    well they've got me quite cross,
    But the sun's been quite kind
    while I wrote this song,
    It's for people like you,
    that keep it turned on.

4. So excuse me forgetting
    but these things I do,
    You see I've forgotten
    if they're green or they're blue,
    Anyway, the thing is,
    what I really mean,
    Yours are the sweetest eyes
    I've ever seen.
    CHORUS

You've Got A Friend

Electronic Organs
Upper: String 8'
Lower: Flutes 8', 4'
Pedal: Electric Bass
Vib./Trem.: On, Fast

Drawbar Organs
Upper: 00 4456 667
Lower:(00) 6332 221
Pedal: String Bass
Vib./Trem.: On, Fast

Words and Music by
Carole King

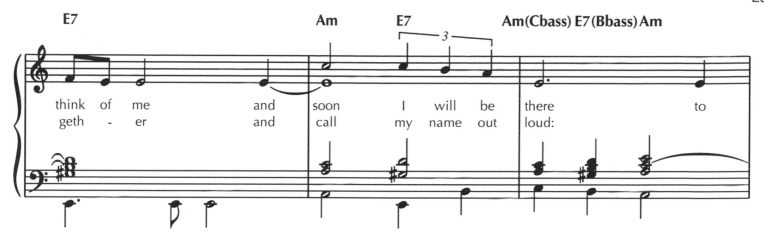

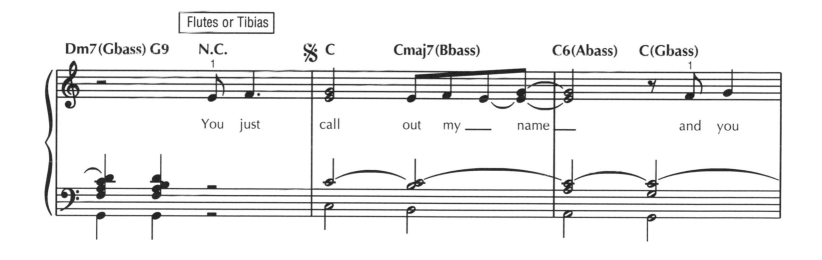

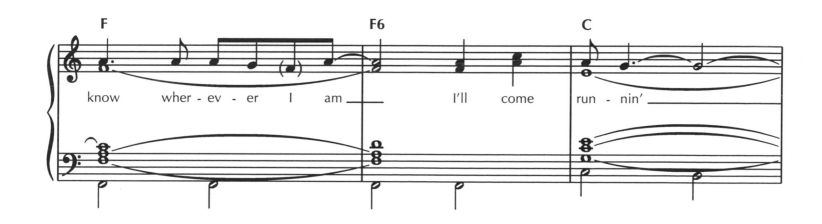

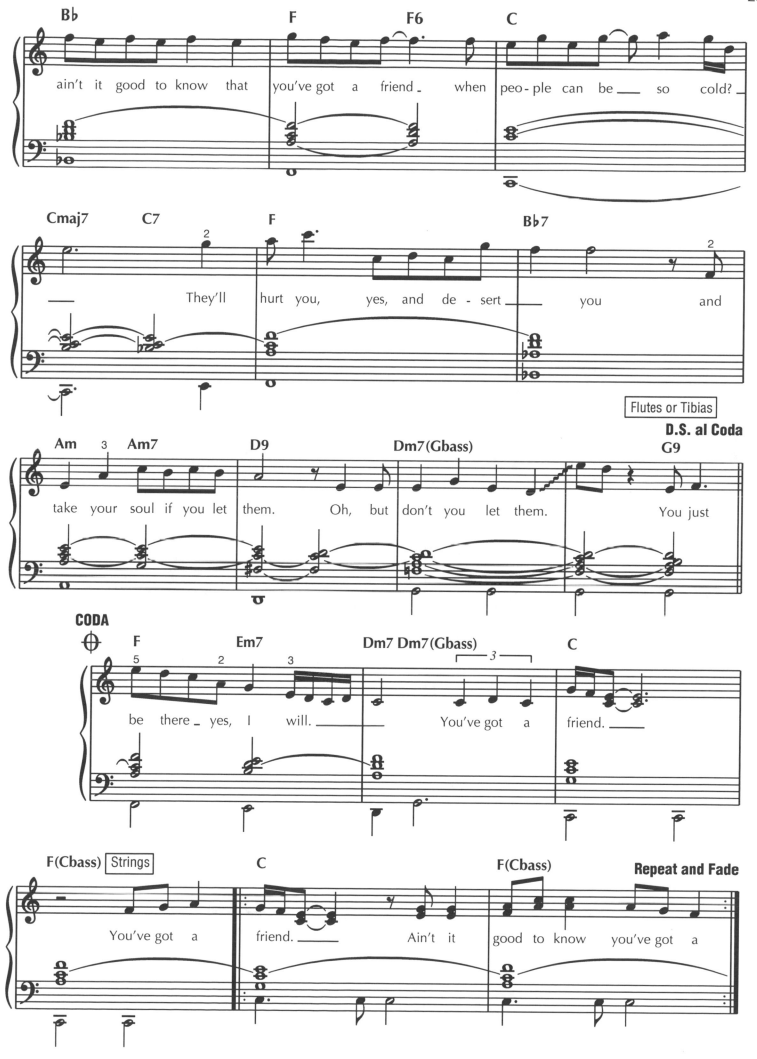

THE BEST SELECTION OF ORGAN MUSIC AVAILABLE

21 Contemporary Love & Wedding Songs
A collection of 21 contemporary romantic songs arranged for all organs. Includes: All I Ask Of You • Endless Love • Friends • Forever And Ever, Amen • Grow Old With Me • Just The Way You Are • So Amazing • Somewhere Out There • Too Much Heaven • Woman • The Velocity Of Love • You Are My Lady • You Needed Me • and more.
00290108 . . . . $8.95

50 Standards For Organ
50 favorite standards, including: Autumn Leaves • The Christmas Song • Hello, Dolly! • I Wanna Be Loved By You • A Good Man Is Hard To Find • Sentimental Journey • One • Unchained Melody • What I Did For Love • Witchcraft • and more.
00290291 . . . . $12.95

105 Favorite Hymns
105 songs arranged by Bill Irwin: Abide With Me • Amazing Grace • Ave Maria • The Church In The Wildwood • Holy, Holy, Holy • Just A Closer Walk With Thee • and more.
00212500 . . . . $10.95

Disney's Beauty And The Beast
Matching songbook to the Disney classic, including: Be Our Guest • Belle • Beauty And The Beast • Something There • and more.
00199109 . . . . $12.95

Irving Berlin Favorites For Organ
Arr. by Dan Rodowicz
23 Berlin favorites, including: Always • Blue Skies • Happy Holiday • I've Got My Love To Keep Me Warm • Puttin' On The Ritz • and many more.
00290251 . . . . $9.95

Christmas Favorites For Organ
24 great songs arranged for organ solo, including: I Heard The Bells On Christmas Day • I'll Be Home For Christmas • Rockin' Around The Christmas Tree • Rudolph The Red-Nosed Reindeer • and more.
00290249 . . . . $9.95

Contemporary Christian Classics
These 12 beloved songs have been arranged for performance on any organ. Music and lyrics are provided for such classics as: Behold The Lamb • El Shaddai • How Majestic Is Your Name • Upon This Rock • We Shall Behold Him • and many more.
00199100 . . . . $6.95

Country Standards For Organ
48 country favorites, including: Another Somebody Done Somebody Wrong Song • Crazy • Forever And Ever, Amen • Grandpa (Tell Me 'Bout The Good Old Days) • If We Make It Through December • Islands In The Stream • Make The World Go Away • Mammas Don't Let Your Babies Grow Up To Be Cowboys • Old Dogs, Children And Watermelon Wine • and many more.
00290228 . . . . $12.95

Easy Classics
arr. Jim Cliff
12 titles for easy organ: Chopin's Nocturne • Emperor Waltz • Jesu, Joy Of Man's Desiring • Ode To Joy (From The Ninth Symphony) • Vienna Life • others.
00276400 . . . . $5.95

Elvis!
40 songs arranged by Jean Tavens: All Shook Up • Don't Be Cruel • Hound Dog • Jail House Rock • Peace In The Valley • Return To Sender • Teddy Bear • Wooden Heart • more. Includes super collection of never-before-published color photos!
00212350 . . . . $12.95

Great Standards For Organ
50 timeless songs, arranged for organ, including: All At Once You Love Her • Call Me • The Entertainer • Goin' Out Of My Head • I Could Write A Book • I'll Be Around • If You Go Away • My Romance • Ol' Man River • Smoke Gets In Your Eyes • Under Paris Skies • Why Do I Love You? • Wonderful! Wonderful! • Younger Than Springtime.
00290207 . . . . $12.95

Latin Organ Favorites
Over 20 Latin favorites, including: Desafinado • The Girl From Ipanema • How Insensitive • More • One Note Samba • Quiet Nights Of Quiet Stars • and more.
00199107 . . . . $9.95

Les Miserables Selections For Organ
14 songs from this smash hit musical including: Bring Him Home • Castle On A Cloud • Do You Hear The People Sing? • I Dreamed A Dream • In My Life • On My Own • and more. Also includes color photos from the Broadway production.
00290270 . . . . $12.95

Disney's The Lion King
Includes all five songs from Disney's smash hit movie *The Lion King*: Be Prepared • Can You Feel The Love Tonight • Circle Of Life • Hakuna Matata • I Just Can't Wait To Be King.
00199110 . . . . $10.95

Phantom Of The Opera
9 of the best songs from the smash hit musical, including: All I Ask Of You • Think Of Me • Wishing You Were Somehow Here Again • and more.
00290300 . . . . $14.95

The Rodgers & Hammerstein All-Organ Book
Over 40 songs from hit Broadway shows, including: Oklahoma! • State Fair • Allegro • South Pacific • The King And I • Pipe Dream • Flower Drum Song • Cinderella • The Sound Of Music.
00312899 . . . . $12.95

Timeless Hits
33 favorites, including: Candle In The Wind • Could I Have This Dance • Forever and Ever Amen • I.O.U. • Just The Way You Are • On Golden Pond • Somewhere Out There • What A Wonderful World • and more.
00199105 . . . . $9.95

FOR MORE INFORMATION, SEE YOUR LOCAL MUSIC DEALER, OR WRITE TO:

HAL•LEONARD® CORPORATION

7777 W. BLUEMOUND RD. P.O. BOX 13819 MILWAUKEE, WI 53213

0797